Noah's Template
of Enterprise
SUCCESS

YINKA AKINTUNDE

Noah's Template
of Enterprise

S U C C E S S

YINKA AKINTUNDE

ResourceHouse

RESOURCE HOUSE LTD
LONDON

†

CatharticVerses.com

First Published 2016 by

RESOURCE HOUSE LTD
resourcehouse@ymail.com
info@diademministries.org
www.diademministries.org
Tel: +44-1708 730085
United Kingdom

All Bible quotations have been taken from the New King James Version of the Bible, unless otherwise indicated in the text. 'KJV' refers to King James Version. 'Amp' refers to Amplified bible. 'NIV' refers to New International Version. 'NLT' refers to New Living Translation.

Printed for Resource House

Contents

Acknowledgement

To the Godhead in person of the Father, Son and the Holy Spirit, from whom all wisdom and inspiration flow, be all glory and thanksgiving.

My precious wife and lovely children, Diadem Church members, Dele Popoola, 'Tunde Fayombo of DigitalKoncepts and every other person and institution who have been a blessing to my person and ministry over time.

God bless you all.

INTRODUCTION

The story of the man Noah in the Bible has generated some blockbuster preaching, teachings and even movies from time immemorial. We are quiet familiar with Noah being the survivor of God's wrath and nature upsurge. Growing up as a child, imagining an 'ordinary' flood wiping off the whole universe was beyond my imagination. Growing up and seeing massive tsunami wiping off cities built in concrete within a twinkle of an eye brought it home to my scientific mind that what was recorded in Noah's case was not only possible but did happen as was said.

Our focus in this book is not the theology of the flood, but the rebuilding of the earth by the survivors. Our objective is to set out a road map for building a successful enterprise from whatever ruin is left as scratch.

Anything can be built or re-built from sub-zero scratch or ruins. Noah serves for us as a role model of a man that had all the chance and excuses to live on water, eat water plants and just hunt water animals for survival. Noah rather than modeling a settler for such comfort zone on water, went on to become a successful farmer and vintner on dry ground against all odds.

I hope you will find light and see hope of starting right or re-starting again after the past ruins. It is my hope you will find success and set a new order of success in your own generation.

CHAPTER 1

WHY ENTERPRISE

That's How It Works Here

The earth was created and meant to be replenished and kept fruitful by human enterprise on it. God will not come down to do a singular thing on earth by Himself again. Having rested already, He had committed the sustenance and keeping of the earth to mankind.

Humanity as a whole and you as an individual will make living, make profit and find fulfilment as we engage this task variously, at different levels and from different angles. The concept of material reward is largely tied to how much an individual is contributing to productivity on earth, either in good, in services or both.

The uphill task of taking on your own share of the project of keeping our world moving and functioning, as best you can and to a profitable end is your enterprise. This will take boldness, readiness of heart, some ingenuity and an adventurous spirit to do most of the times.

Up until now, our world has been making strides in progress through the spirit of enterprise resident in man. From science to finance, politics, sport and any other value adding adventure on earth. people have taken the bull by the horns and made something significant out of what they met on ground. We are where we are today, enjoying what we are enjoying today in goods and services simply because someone took part of the earth projects as his or her own enterprise.

"The uphill task of taking on your own share of the project of keeping our world moving and functioning, as best you can and to a profitable end is your enterprise".

Suffice to say is that fact that profitability marks out every successful enterprise. Profits can be in material or immaterial forms and can be both. Tangible and intangible profiting of the earth by mankind is what culminates to what we call development today. All effort invested by man for evolvement of the earth today are all we reap as the modern world. We are reaping these enterprising endeavours in food, clothing, transportation, aviation, medicine, space exploration, information technology and many more wonderful areas of human needs and desires. We are reaping on land in the air and on the sea. We are reaping as individual and collectively the fruits of what humanity at various times and ages had taken on as enterprise so far.

A Part to Play

> And Noah began to be a farmer, and he planted a vineyard. Genesis 9:20.

Aside the post-flood breeding of the new human race, Noah was saddled with the serious task of setting the pace for the reconstruction of the devastated world. He needed to boldly forgo the possible loneliness his family would probably have been subjected to, having been the only surviving clan of mankind after the flood. Being the only surviving family in the entire earth would definitely have come with the attending temptation of depression. He could have started a blame game when the reality of being alone in massive globe of mere receding water and some dry ground hit home.

Noah's sons were newly wedded I suppose, as they had no children yet. Their wives and even Noah's wife had nobody in their own maiden lineage around again. Except in a movie, the prospect of being the only family in a city is not attractive talk less of in the whole wide world. Noah had no competitor either for land or in business. He had to be self-motivated and well driven to make something great out of his present reality. We are not told what sort of business Noah was doing before he 'found grace' but one thing we were sure was that he wasn't selling arks. Whatever therefore became of Noah's pre-flood business we don't know, but we are sure that his old business did not survive the flood.

Noah had a choice of allowing his mind to drift along these several paths of least resistance and much more, but he rather chose to be productive. He could have started picking fishes and other stranded marine animals left ashore by the flood for survival but he chose to be productive. He could have left the dispersion of seeds to natural forces like wind, water, birds and other animals. But he realised that such chance taking adventure of leaving things to nature would not only be slow and bedeviled with various uncertainties, the place of yielding may not be within his reach of reaping. He also knew that choice would be violated when life is left too much to mere happenstance. He would not have been able to control which kind of seed is majorly cultivated relative to the others, and it would have been difficult to also measure progress.

Taking the bull by the horn is the force behind the enterprising spirit needed for profiting here on the earth. When you see the so called global village as your village of enterprise, it will position you in the place of responsibility. Taking on the responsibilities diligently, wisely and responsibly brings you to the place of profiting. When you profit considerably to the point of relevance, it will create for you a platform of reckoning. Many inventors, innovators and other dwellers of the earth, past and present, are in the place of positive reckoning today because of their involvement in the global enterprise. Some in the enterprise of service delivery in leadership like Winston Churchill came up when the Europe needed resistance to a bloody villain as Adolf Hitler. The Wright brothers, Isaac Newton, Michael Faraday and many more easily come to mind as people who improved how we live today by their spirit of enterprise.

Your personal enterprise has a crucial part to play in the evolvement and development of the global enterprise just as a little block of piece to a puzzle. Personal enterprise can be part of a larger enterprise such as being a nurse or doctor in a hospital. It could be as sole or part owner of an organisation, such as an entrepreneur or a partnership. Whichever form it takes; you need to bring something to the table of productivity in whatever relevant shape or form. To this end will there be personal and collective profiting with the replenishing of the earth continuing as intended at creation. What you cannot afford to be or do is to sit back, fold your hands and expect the

> The heaven, even the heavens, is the LORD's; but the earth He has given to the children of men.
> Psalm 115:16

earth to build itself or for God to do it for you.

A Reward to Get
Development and evolvement in any system are subject to risk when rewards are no more the functions of profitable input. Your rewards here on earth are therefore mostly a function of your enterprise engagement. Whether you are being rewarded in wages, salary or even with political office; you must have done something to merit reward.

Even though what you are and who you are important and can determine what you do; nevertheless, you are mostly rewarded here on earth based on what you do. Having a lofty degree in a field does not translate to being rewarded in cash or kind in that field. No organisation pays you salary and bonuses based on your resume; you are rewarded in accordance to your input into that organisation. We have celebrated who and what we are enough; it is time to start dwelling on what we do. Many parts of the world today suffer greatly from ineffective and ill-effective leadership because; leadership in their concept is what and who you are and not what you do. So we see tragedy of leaders doing everything and anything possible to occupy positions only for that art of ascending the throne to be the best effort they could offer humanity. After ascension, the rest is mediocrity and poor work ethics galore; yet the crave to remain in office for the personality it confers is unabated.

Noah began to be a farmer and was rewarded with harvest and a winery because he planted a vineyard. *Being a farmer does not bring harvest*, planting and cultivating as a farmer do.

Your total worth in material and non-material wealth here on earth, outside of inheritance, is a function of what you are ultimately rewarded with over the period of your productivity. Since worthy inheritance is not certain for all, it is time to start your own venture into productivity. Noah was a man with nothing to inherit as the world, including whatever he had inherited from his own lineage had just been wiped off the earth.

> Moreover, the profit of the earth is for all: the king himself is served by the field.
> Ecclesiastes 5:9

There is a tendency to keep looking at the 'lucky ones' and the 'privileged ones' of the earth and keep writing your own self out of the equation of the 'haves'. The truth is that even the 'lucky' and the 'privileged' ones are dependent on their continuous profitability with whatever they have on the earth or else they go bankrupt and soon be so unlucky. This profiting or reward is available to all; we are told above. You might not have started at the same level and with the same privilege as the others but you can start wherever you are and go forward. Noah started from the place of clean slate, wiped clean by flood with not enough staff members to work for him. He had no buyers to buy his farm produce either. But whatever the world is today started from the adventures of Noah in post-flood enterprise.

Your past efforts may have been wiped off by flood of failure, depression or recession; you can start again and make success out of your new venture. The then world was wiped because of the evil of the inhabitants thereof. In like manner, your past failure may be due to your bad deeds and wrong decisions. It makes no difference anymore; the earth is established for profiting. As long as you live on it, do not give up on profiting. Rewards are tied to your adventure in enterprise, either as a small unit in a larger enterprise or as an entrepreneur working on your own, you just need to be doing something.

A World to Build

There was an earth to be re-built. No one would live there but Noah and his descendants, so Noah needed to smell the coffee and wake up to the task. There is a world, in fact your own world, you need to build. No politician or church will really build your world for you as it was intended to be built. I am sure angels were on earth in the days of Noah as ministering spirits to him who was an inheritor of grace, yet they didn't build the world for him. Every other contributor in your world is a helper, whether they are spirits or human, including the Holy Spirit. Everyone is building

> Every other contributor in your world is a helper, whether they are spirits or human, including the Holy Spirit.

his or her own world within the context and larger picture of the entire world, physical and spiritual. What you build is what you eventually inhabit and enjoy. No institution will build your world for you; you will. Governments can create an enabling and secure environment; schools can give you formal training in skill acquisition, but they cannot do the bigger part of the project for you, which is you taking on life as a project. The church can create a good and inspiring atmosphere for you to access God's blessing; an anointed minister can impart you with grace for building aright, but neither of these can do the bigger job therein for you. Even God's involvement in how you build your world is premised upon and is a function of how much you are doing in building it.

> For every house is built by someone, but He who built all things is God.
> Hebrews 3:4

Why Noah

Be there and be counted, if you are spared.

Noah was spared by grace and so he took his chance and maximized his moment. We cannot discountenance the existence of tragedies and unfortunate situations which daily assail the natural but fallen world. Whenever they happen, they do not only threatened but most certainly takeaway survival from their victims. Sicknesses, disabilities, natural and manmade disasters such as war and many more rank highs among such tragedies. For the victims, enterprise is likely not one of the major issues that will come up in their priority lists.

But if you are privileged to be reading and can comprehend this writing, then you are a spared breed. You probably have gone through dangers and distress but if you have been spared, get productive. You were not spared to play the victim and live as one for the rest of your life; you were spared to rebuild your world. Many were drowned in the same water you rode to this dry ground. It took a long time for the water to recede but at least you are now on dry ground. You might have had to be kept in the ark for a while, but now you have been let loose to bring forth.

If you have survived your own flood, it is time to bring forth. I am talking of the flood of abuse and discriminations. The flood you survived may be of past failure and mistakes. It could be the flood of alcoholism, broken marriage, past drug abuse and the worst of habits out there. If you have survived it, then get up and prove it. Prove that the flood has a survivor. Prove that you are now on dry ground by

Prove that you are now on dry ground by cultivating the ground. Let what is left of and for you become the capital platform of bringing forth the great possibilities resident within, yet hidden and veiled away from your waiting world.

cultivating the ground. Let what is left of and for you become the capital platform of bringing forth the great possibilities resident within, yet hidden and veiled away from your waiting world.

It Is In You

And Noah began to be a farmer – Genesis 9:20a

And he planted a vineyard – Genesis 9:20b.

I decided to divide this verse into two parts so that you can appreciate how things work in our world. Noah was rewarded with harvest to the point of building the first recorded wine factory, simply because he planted a vineyard. But before he successfully planted a vineyard, Noah began '*to be*' a farmer. He was rewarded based on what he did, but he did what he did based on who he was.

When you live in a world of make-believe like ours, where a lot of people are actors/actresses of some sort, it is easy to fall prey of what look like glittering ends being paraded without looking at state of the means. Noah's testimony of success started in him. The productivity was resident in his person. He was something first and then did something, before he then had something.

The inherent law of productivity is that *everyone*

produces after his or her own kind. What kind you are in the inside has a lot to do with what you do in the outside and what you have in the end. What is in your hands as skill or resources are very crucial in productivity but they are not as crucial as what is in you. Yes, where you are located can really play a role in your productivity. Indeed, God talks of certain lands as flowing with milk and honey, but where you are located is not as important as what is located in you.

See this illustration. Give nine amateurs and one top professional golfer the same kits and same course to play, and bring in a group of judges to assess them. After a while, without prior knowledge of who is who, the judges will be able to point out the professional from the amateur, both in approach and in results. This will be so even if they are all of the same height, frame and have the same garments on, including masks to hide their identities. Who you are in the intrinsic sense matters beyond what you are in the outside. This brings us back to Vintner Noah. He was all that in the inside and thus successful in the outside because of what happened to him along the way. Noah found grace. I will not want us to look at this grace in theological sense here. Let us just see it in the context of Noah's destiny or assignment. In essence we can say that part of *what Noah found as grace was not just the mercy to escape the flood but an endowment to live beyond and after the flood.*

You are endowed in one area or the other to make living worth it for you. Your endowment may need some formal education and certificate to come to fore, but you are endowed. Your endowment may be in tangible or intangible talents or gifts, but you are endowed. In every human is that first and basic instalment of grace necessary for productivity. When you look inward, you will discover why you have been spared so far. When you start being what you are endowed to be, you will start doing what you are gifted to do and the start having result as you ought to have.

Salient points to consider:

- Bring out your endowments
- Meet your needs
- Meet the needs of others
- Be rewarded
- Create opportunities for others
- Bring out the endowments in others
- Find fulfilment(s)
- Make choice(s)
- Look inward

CHAPTER

2

THE
INTANGIBLE
CAPITAL
OF GRACE

Capital in Perspective

Capital is not a new concept, native only to the modern world. Since productivity began, capital has always been a major pillar. Capital in the context of enterprise is any material and non-material input whether in quantifiable or non-quantifiable measure invested in production of goods or services to the end of reaping back commensurate output in higher value. We are mostly familiar with money as a form of capital for enterprise. Truly money is a capital, but many people have brought only their skills as capital into an organisation and have become stakeholders there, being rewarded back in cash and kind based on their input of skills. Whatever you bring to the market place of life as input in exchange for more value in output is your capital. To make gain is for the value realised as product to be higher than the input, while to make loss is the exact opposite.

"Capital in the context of enterprise is any material and non-material input whether in quantifiable or non-quantifiable measure invested in production of goods or services to the end of reaping back commensurate output in higher value."

This now brings up the concept of value. Capital is value deposit that brings back value to us in its multiplied forms, once it goes through the line of production. Capital can be tangible and it can be intangible. Learning from Noah's enterprise, many values were brought into Noah's production line as capital before he became such a successful farmer worthy of reckoning. Noah probably had no money, and even if he did, money would have been of no value at that material time. The issue would have been a question of what would Noah buy with money and from whom would he?

If for whatever reason our world today has only one family as the occupants, the first thing that would happen is that the concept of demand and supply will crash immediately. For lack of competitive trade, all stocks will crash, from NYSE to FTSE, Dow Jones and all other major global platforms there are. All currency will worth less than the paper they

"Tangible capital only has value that is demand driven."

were printed with for lack of demand. So therefore, tangible capital only has value that is demand driven.

All capital that are demand driven are not absolute in themselves; they are relative in value and subject to devaluation. They are dependent on external value-determining factors and their places are in productivity and not necessarily in their intrinsic worth. As valuable as gold is, its value fluctuates based on this principle. Even skill as a value, it being a form of tangible capital, is driven to some extent by the external value and milieu. That is why being a medical doctor in one part of the world may be of greater value as capital than in another part. This value realisation and other factors drive skill and investment migrations across the globe.

The world recently witnessed a global recession *(between 2007-2009)* in which values were eroded off what were the monetary valuation of companies in stocks. I chose to make this reference so that you can see the limitation of tangible capital. Supposing you are caught in a web of personal or global economic adversity that takes tangible capital value off your hand, you need to know what to do for recovery. On the other hand, it may even be an outright drought of monetary capital needed for your enterprise to take off, you need to know how to realise value from intangible capital you have got.

In the course of pastoring and leading Christian organisations from my undergraduate days, to interacting with families and friends on enterprise across the world, I have found out that the major culprit which accusing finger has been pointed at the most for not showing up when needed is *capital*. Apart from the absence of efficient public system, lack of capital is almost the most blamed cause by intending entrepreneurs or otherwise of not doing what they would have loved to do. *(I used the term otherwise here because there is an erroneous teaching that allude to a belief system that all enterprising endeavours must be entrepreneurial. This is not true but all productive efforts must be enterprising. This could be sole enterprise, partnership in its various forms or enterprise within a bigger enterprise).* When such people say that there is no capital, money is what they implicitly refer to most of the time. *In as much as we cannot undermine what money can do as a capital, we need to know that money is a value that has a pattern of showing up*. When we master this pattern, we can create value that will compel money to eventually show up as capital when and where it is needed.

Most of the very profitable and valuable ventures on earth today were not started with loads of money. Silicon Valley in California is probably the richest land mass in term of the cumulative global value created by the companies there. Most of those very valuable companies were not started with money-capital; they attracted money-capital latter on, having traded with some other capital to a point of reckoning for a while.

This brings up back to our subject, Noah. He obviously didn't have much material capital the day he disembarked the ark. The concept of demand and supply capital market was out of place in this scenario. Noah did not even start off with tangible capital.

Instead, Noah started building his enterprise empire with non-tangible capital. In the course of this, he was able to realise the full value of whatever tangible things he could lay hold of as capital.

> Much food is in the tillage of the poor: but there is that is destroyed for want of judgment.
> Proverbs 13:23

Many have ended up locking up the treasure of productivity in them to obvious lack of material starting point. Lack of judgement above means to wrongly appraise one's circumstance and situation based on a wrong evaluating system in the inside. Some have taken lack of formal education or lack of some kind of skin colour or background as a major absence of capital to take off in life. If you put a ghetto mind in a mansion in an urbane upscale part of the city, two of the many horrible eventualities will happen. It either will go back to ghetto where it fits in or transform the place to ghetto to fit in, as long as its inner appraisal of life does not change. Value adding and value creating minds can never lack capital for profiting whether tangible or intangible. You need to sit back now and appraise what you have. This I believe was what Noah did and he hit the salvo of productivity.

I will like us to look at *eight major capitals in Noah's*

disposal after the flood. Five of them are intangible, and we shall see them in the next five chapters. The other three are tangible capital which we shall see in the subsequent three chapters.

Intangible Capital of Grace

The first question Noah would have kept on asking himself, when he was asked to build an Ark against all obvious odds would have been the common question of *'why me'*. We were not told that Noah had any ecclesiastic background. He was not a Pastor neither was he a preacher of any sort. Noah was just another man out there whose ways and values aligned with that of God to a satisfactory level, based on divine standard of godliness set for his own dispensation, time and generation. With the understandable ridicules and challenges from others around him, Noah could not stop doing the obviously ridiculous in the name of following God. He rather followed that inner urge to do the unpopular. I am sure the question would have been asked repeatedly and much more during the flood as he watched everything wiped off the earth with awe. Noah would have probably seen his old friends and neighbours swept past his ark both young and old and would have asked again and again, why him in there and not them. Having survived the flood, the day Noah came out of the ark and few days afterward would have been surreal days of retrospection and introspection. Noah, being not so self-righteous, would probably have recalled how nothing in human rights terminology had qualified him for such benevolence of heaven. At one point or the other, Noah would have then come to the conclusion that it was *'grace'* that found him.

Grace in the context of this book is either the natural or supernatural benevolence bestowed on you as endowments. There was a deposit of benevolent endowment in Noah even before the script of the flood started playing out. In like manner, there is a dimension of natural endowments in you *simply because you are human*, and that is a measure of grace. If you have taken a step further into the saving grace through Christ Jesus, you are now talking of being naturally endowed as human and supernaturally endowed as a regenerated spirit.

- *Grace Capital as Natural Endowments:* There personalities that we didn't pay a dime nor even did a second of training for to have. Many are in activism, politics, military, show business and various other human endeavours today because being and doing such thing is naturally resident and at home in them as endowments. Being human on its own is a natural endowment and a capital of grace which puts us on the platform and in the line of productivity. We think the way we do and want to coordinate other creatures and objects on the earth because we are human. Noah saw this advantage he had over elephants even though the elephant was bigger than he was. He saw it as a grace he could take to the market place of life. Being human means all other creations can be made to work to our advantage. Noah saw this grace and took it.

Your being human is a capital of grace; use it to your advantage. People have made good ventures in fashion out of them wanting to be clothed in certain ways and thus end up creating lines and trends in fashion market. People have leveraged on a kind of food, spice, drink or condiment they love and have taste for to create a profitable food company. People have been given roles that brought them fame and wealth because of the tone and texture of their voices. For some, it is because of their gender. Many because of their height, some because of their weight or body build. Your capital starts with your natural endowments, only if you will see and capitalise on them. Martin Luther King Jnr.'s greatness started from him being a black man which didn't come across as an advantage in his days. If Luther king had been a white man, he wouldn't have suited the role he played nor had the value he had. He would have just been one of the many in the crowd, even if he had had sympathy for the black race and had helped in the emancipation. *You can realise the capital of grace in who you are naturally rather than struggling to be something else.* No matter how clever or strong, no other being except humans could do what Noah did in his days. People make a lot of enterprise from other creatures such as animals in our world today, but no other creation can do that but man.

- ***Grace Capital as Supernatural Endowment:*** Till the days of Noah, there had never been rain neither had anyone built an ark before. It would have taken Noah some supernatural endowments to see what God was showing and also to follow through accurately. There had been hunters like Nimrod before Noah was born and so the concept of wild animals was not strange. To bring these entire wild animals into the ark would have been naturally impossible. The whole concept of the capital of grace as supernatural endowment is therefore relevant here: when God in His benevolence is making up for what you are short of through Christ Jesus. When enablement to achieve results is being granted you from on high. When you are being helped over and above what would have been hindrances and your natural limit. When you are being marked up by heaven because you have not scored enough on your own to get the enterprise done. I remember my pre-clinic days in the medical college, the exams could be so tough at times that no one did really pretty well in the real sense of it. The examination board would then do what is called 'marking up the scripts'. They would look for a fairly good mark that the reasonable size of the class had scored up to or above and make it the cut off mark. Because the pass mark was always 50%, they would calculate the difference between the cut off chosen and 50, this would be the mark-up. It would be added to everyone's original score and the result would then be released. Many who eventually passed would probably have failed if not for the benevolent providence of 'marking up' by the faculty. Same thing is done by any good trader who wants to make profit. Having bought the good at a cost, whatever level of profit in expectation will then be added to the cost price as mark-up to determine the selling price.

Now That You Are Marked Up

Just like our gracious examiners then, or like a trader trying to make profit, God has added enough mark-up of help to you through new birth in Christ so that you don't come back empty or with loss from the market place of life. Grace means all you need for life and godliness with all the attending profiting in the temporal and eternal life has been given and incorporated into your new life.

You have divine help as capital; you must capitalise on it. Many like you have come to the market place of life with nothing but divine help *(Grace of God)* and made good use of their space. You need to go out there like a well helped victor and not as helpless victim. Grace marks up for the inequality in human system and the circumstantial disadvantages in your cost. Noah had grace capital and he knew it. He succeeded with it and became the pioneer saint of every man or woman involved in one enterprise or the other out there who has also found grace and wants profit. Grace is a major capital for profiting; use it. Remain gracious as your profiting starts showing up. Be gracious with gratitude, be gracious with humility. Grace means it could have been someone else who was given the privilege.

THE
INTANGIBLE
CAPITAL
OF THE WORD

CHAPTER 3

Imagine a world where all of us are deaf and dumb, with no communication at all in spoken words. The limit to the evolvement of humanity would have been so enormous. Human have been able to make so many strides because of our capacity to send words on errand and receive words as errand. People have spoken their ways into and out of wealth over time in human history. Nations have spoken themselves into and out of war, debt, victories and defeats severally and variously.

People mostly attend interviews to speak themselves into a job or out of a job and career opportunity. For

Noah, he heard the words spoken to him by God into productivity and he took it as capital for enterprise with which he prospered. I will therefore narrow the word here to the word of God. This could be the general concept of God's mind as 'logos' or the specific mind of God spoken for a purpose and time as 'rhema'. In either case, both have the capacity to become flesh or tangible value for you in the market.

> **Then God spoke to Noah, saying, go out of the ark, you and your wife, and your sons and your sons' wives with you. Bring out with you every living thing of all flesh that is with you: birds and cattle and every creeping thing that creeps on the earth, so that they may abound on the earth, and be fruitful and multiply on the earth. So Noah went out, and his sons and his wife and his sons' wives with him. Every animal, every creeping thing, every bird, and whatever creeps on the earth, according to their families, went out of the ark. Genesis 8:15-19**

The capital of divine instruction can never be undervalued in the enterprise of anyone who has something to do with God. Like I said earlier, this can be general or specific. I did not call this capital the intangible capital of divine instruction because I don't want your mind to be abused with prejudice and shot down the horizon as regarding divine instruction. Neither do I want you to start looking for dreams and voices and miss the whole concept of divine instruction. So keeping it simple, let's call the capital of divine instruction Noah used and profited with as *the word capital*.

Noah building and going into the ark was premised on divine instruction. Who he brought and what he took in were not who and what he just wanted to bring and take in. They were who and what he was asked to bring in. When Noah came out of the ark, he did so because he was told to do so. What he was to do when he came out was also given to him as instruction as we can see in the above scripture. Noah was told to do the following:

(i)   *Go out of the ark.*
(ii)   *Go out with all your family who were with you.*
(iii)   *Bring out all the living things that were with you.*
(iv)   *Bring them (every living thing) out so they can massively increase eventually.*

Noah's mandate was simple and straight forward, and it created direction for his next endeavour. Knowing where to go and what to do is a major capital itself in the world of enterprise. It conserves your resources and energy, including time. It narrows down your field of resource investment.

Noah knew the human and animals would probably mate naturally by urge for intimacy and kept bringing forth but the plants would likely not do same in orderly and productive manner. Based on mandate (iv) above, Noah took advantage of the instruction and started being a farmer. His last known job was that of a ship builder, sailor and administrator. But based on availability of instruction as a capital, he went into farming enterprise.

What you need as capital at this juncture may not be yet another degree, it may not be money, and it may not even be applying for a new job or starting a new business. You may just need to watch out for instruction. Bear it in mind that you are configured to pick up signals of instruction in your inside already by the virtue of your new birth

.

You are able to know what to do even if you have to feel your way like a blind folded man and miss a few steps. Your being instructed does not have to be eventful and dramatic, you are not out to prove any point of hyper-spirituality - are you? You simply need a nudge by God through his word that is resident in you as light to know where to invest your other capitals.

The fear and question of whether the plants would bring forth or not were allayed and answered as far as Noah was concerned once he saw God's word as the law of life that must be obeyed. He knew that the living seeds he was about to start planting too heard God when God said all living should bring forth, multiply and replenish the earth. Before Noah laid hold of any tangible capital of seed, he knew that behind his business enterprise was the intangible capital of the word of divine instruction.

This word was a law to be obeyed by everything, living and non-living he reckoned. He knew the other living things too heard the word and so would not do anything to jeopardise his plantings. He knew that the animals would rather add manure to his plants rather than destroy them. There is a capital of confidence infused into your enterprise when you know that you are within the confines of divine instruction. This could be the general instruction simply written in God's word or specific instruction backed up by the law of the spirit of life in Christ Jesus.

THE
INTANGIBLE
CAPITAL
OF BLESSING

CHAPTER 4

Blessing is divine force released in words to compel every force in existence to work for the advancement and advantage of the blessed. This includes spiritual, human and natural forces. The spiritual force can even be that of light or darkness. When blessing is at work, everything is compelled to make things work for the blessed. The exact opposite happens when there is a curse at work.

> And God blessed Noah and his sons, and said unto them, be fruitful, and multiply, and replenish the earth. And the fear of you and the dread of you shall be upon every beast of the earth, and upon every fowl of the air, upon all that moves upon the earth, and upon all the fishes of the sea; into your hand are they delivered. Every moving thing that lives shall be meat for you; even as the green herb have I given you all things; Genesis 9:1-3.

Before Noah started any venture after the flood, God had to bless him with the kind of blessing Adam had in the beginning. The blessing was like an insurance to guarantee that whatever Noah was going to do based on the instruction he had earlier had would prosper and be secured.

Water body, wind body, pest or animal and any force there present in the then world could do nothing but work to the advantage and advancement of Noah. He was blessed and he knew it. He had the capital of blessing and knew it. He knew his plant would be compelled to bring forth on the visible realm ruled by the unseen force of blessing. Blessing is an intangible force that compels tangible manifestation of positive results in the hands of its carrier; *Proverbs 10:22*. We talk of Abraham, Isaac and Jacob as epitome of people who started out on various ventures with blessing as the main capital deposits and ended up with rich organization at last. Surely they did, but long before any of them showed up on the scene had Noah showed us that blessing is a good capital to start with.

Blessing will bring everything to eventually work to your advantage and change your state of being until you are what the blessing describes you to be. It will not only change your being and experience to such, it will also defend you in that state against any negative force that wants to work against it.

Blessing Provokes Angelic Help

The capital of blessing comes with angelic help on any venture it rests upon. There are values beyond the realm of man and visible entities that bear their weight on the eventual outcome of human efforts in life. The dream of Jacob at Bethel and one of his experiences at the house of Laban show us that the angels of God work with the blessed as ministering spirits. *Genesis 28:10- 19; Genesis 31:1-13.*

Angels are busy ascending with requests and descending with help on the enterprise of the blessed to make sure everything works well. They are agents of light and so repel evil forces of darkness which would want to work against your success. They go ahead and with you for interviews and into board meetings. They compel circumstances and situations to turn out well for you as you engage the outside world in your venture and enterprise. Angels will help you in publicity as they announced the birth of Jesus to the three wise men; they will compel the right clients into your direction because you have the blessing capital to work with.

Blessing Is Resourceful

Blessing as capital has creative ability, which means it can bring resources out of nothing for you. It also has multiplier effect, which means it will multiply the resources which you have and make them increased greatly.

When I left home and crossed the Jordan River, I owned nothing except a walking stick. Now my household fills two large camps. Genesis 32:10b (NLT).

That was the testimony of brother Jacob, a man who started his enterprise with blessing capital principally.

CHAPTER 5

THE INTANGIBLE CAPITAL OF FAITH

The whole adventure of life for Noah from that point when God gave him the task of building an ark was premised on faith walk.

> By faith Noah, being divinely warned of things not yet seen, moved with godly fear, prepared an ark for the saving of his household, by which he condemned the world and became heir of the righteousness which is according to faith
>
> Hebrews 11:7

For Noah, faith was more than a mere belief system; it was not just a feeling of spirituality; faith for Noah was *'a moving'*. It was an action or some actions. Faith for Noah was a visible action of dancing to the tune of music from an invisible God. Noah showed God and the entirety of creation that he believed both the words and blessing of God earlier discussed by putting up some actions. He started moving things and cultivating things, just as he was building an ark earlier on, simply because he believed.

Faith for enterprise is a doing faith, not a wishing faith. Talk is cheap, faith is hard work. Let us see the two parts of faith that is needed here.

(I)   **Believing:**   God deals in covenants of promises; it takes the believing ones to line up for the benefits there. God had just said to Noah that he would not destroy the world with flood again and that sowing will always yield harvest over time. Noah had a simple belief system and acted back in response to same. Do not complicate your faith for enterprise, simply act out your belief.

(II)   **Trust:** For Noah, faithful was he that promised him multiplication, who would also do it. He trusted God's integrity to make real His promises. The risks he took were the risks he knew God had insured in the covenant. You also need to do your own part and leave the remaining performance to God.

With your doing faith, you can throw your net at the Lord's instruction for net breaking harvest of fishes where you had been toiling before.

Faith capital links up your enterprise to the ability of God to perform. It positions your endeavours for supernatural experience.

"Faith capital links up your enterprise to the ability of God to perform."

CHAPTER

THE INTANGIBLE CAPITAL OF FATE

Oh yes, fate is a capital for the discerning. By fate here we mean inevitable and unavoidable happenstance of life. I know that when you had been well schooled in faith, the tendency to discountenance fate is huge. You need to know that certain events of life are beyond our choice and control whether we like it or not. These are circumstances we cannot change; God in his infinite ability has made them rigid. Trying to change them will always result in catastrophe of immeasurable consequences. Wisdom here is to see the capital in such situation and maximise their use.

Noah found himself in an unfortunate situation of being the sole occupier of the whole wide world. Instead of bemoaning his fate, he took advantage of unlimited access to land to start farming. If what happened had not happen he might not have had access to the land as much as he did after the flood. Poor geographical location, a dysfunctional family background, the gloomy global economy or even catastrophe of disastrous proportion may be the turning point you need to spur you into your enterprise pursuit. Many pharmaceutical companies today owe their breakthrough to one outbreak of disease or the other. Penicillin was discovered by accident, many companies feed fat on various variants of it today under different brand names and modifications.

People have stumbled so to say on career, partnership or even entrepreneurial opportunities by chance and made great enterprises out of same. Your ability to spot and seize the moment is a capital beyond mountain of gold. Facebook being one of the modern day fate at work was not started out to be a multibillion enterprise, but someone saw the capital of chance and took it. The rest is history.

There was a young man by the name Joseph in the Egyptian prison some centuries ago. He happened to be around when there was going to be a serious famine. The summary of Joseph's story was that he leveraged on the unfortunate global drought and made money for his boss, Pharaoh. He became rich and influential too in doing so; *Genesis 47:13-26*. The not so funny side of fate in the story was that some people including women and children would have died of hunger in the course of the famine. People have made good careers in the military because of war. As good and globally profitable as the concept of the internet is today, both in direct information technology business and allied use, it was a product of war. It was developed for the United States Department of Defense. The decision to commission a research along this line was probably born of the army's experience in Second World War as regards communication.

> "Fate that you cannot change may be a call into the higher life of making enterprise out of managing same."

Fate becomes a capital once it spurs the desire to make good things out of bad or better out of good in you. You can take that desire to the market place of life and convert it to action and currency eventually. People have used the bad childhood experiences which they have had no control over as fate leverage for global impact. In bringing help and giving voice to other victims, they have found their own voices and greatly helped themselves.

Salient Points to Consider:

- It takes value investment to reap back value.
- Capital means value to be invested in order to reap back higher value.
- Intangible capital is real and must be your starting point in creating tangible value.
- Natural and supernatural endowments of grace must be invested as capital for profiting.
- Instruction is a capital that creates direction of investment of your other forms of capital.
- Blessing is a creative capital.
- It is faith capital only when it is acted upon in the market place.
- Good or bad fate can become a launching pad or beckoning opportunity to be harvested.

CHAPTER 7

THE TANGIBLE CAPITAL OF RELATIONSHIP

TANGIBLE CAPITAL

As real and important as your intangible capital are, they need tangible channels of expressions in order for you to have rewards of value in the market place. Noah understood this concept well and so he gave maximum place of priority to his tangible capital as much as he did of the intangible ones. Trying to overlook the place of your tangible capital is to be building a castle in the air in the name of a career enterprise. It is a serious malady among people of faith to assume that prayer as a so called master key will do everything for us.

The bitter reality is that there is no master key in life. If there were any, Jesus Christ would have said so but he didn't even make any inference close to that. He rather gave us keys of the kingdom. He mentioned keys but no master key. The problem with us is that we want to do in one day what God did in six. Preachers may tell you that there is a cure- it-all formula to apply to life, but there is none. The master himself applied different keys with different approach as the situations warranted. If there was anyone who should just have used one key to unlock the whole process of creation at one moment, and in one day, that should be God. He should have done so because he could do so, but he chose not to do so to set a pattern for us.

Not only did God decide not to just call forth creation into existence at once in a moment, he also didn't do it in a single day. God chose the task for each day and used the right tool. He had been using same tool for five days until the sixth day when he wanted to create man. This time he didn't just use the intangible capital of his word and power; he brought to bear the skill capital of moulding and the material capital of clay. This shows us that the most spiritual amongst us should still have respect for tangible capital if you really want to build a successful enterprise.

Faith, favour, fasting, prayers, blessing and grace put together can never replace the cardinal of tangible capital in your pursuit of a successful enterprise. Intangible capital can help you to realise the value of your tangible capitals but they cannot replace them for you. Let us have a closer look at *the three forms of tangible capital* in the hand of Noah.

THE TANGIBLE CAPITAL OF RELATIONSHIP
(Social Capital)

Good will is a capital. It can purchase value than money can do in its infinite quantity. Noah was the righteous one but he did not go into the ark alone, neither was he commanded to come out alone. In fact, the mandate of multiplication was not given to him alone but to all the living things with him, including the creeping things. His journey out of the ark started when he partnered with the raven and doves to do some reconnaissance flights to assess how dry and safe the land was for the ark to land.

> Then God spoke to Noah, saying, go out of the ark, you and your wife, and your sons and your sons' wives with you. Bring out with you every living thing of all flesh that is with you: birds and cattle and every creeping thing that creeps on the earth, so that they may abound on the earth, and be fruitful and multiply on the earth. So Noah went out, and his sons and his wife and his sons' wives with him. Genesis 8:15-19.

God kept using the phrase 'you and' so that it would be clear to Mr. Noah that relationship counted there and then. God also said 'bring out with you' so that Noah would be conscious of the fact that he was in it with others and not alone.

When we start paying close attention to relationships, we will start realising capital value beyond what we can pay for with money. Moderately talented and skillful people have come under the capital influence of coaches and managers who had their lives turned around in a greater way than their skills or talent could afford. Whereas we have seen many hugely talented people with lots of potentials miss out in greatness due to lack of the right relationships. Relationships can open doors to showcase the skill capital in you and can shut the same doors. It can build platforms for the exposure and can crash the existing platforms.

Joseph was introduced to the palace by the butler he had a good relationship with, no matter how belated. I believe Moses was allowed the chance to grow up in the palace by God so as to build some kind of relationships necessary for access for him ahead of his days of manifestation. He could have been killed by palace guards while trying to see Pharaoh even before his anointing was demonstrated before leaders of the land in the battle of snakes. People unknown in political circles have used the leverage of relationships here and there to build political enterprises which have allowed them to eventually become global leaders and strong political figures. No matter how noble your idea is, someone may have to leverage you or else you may die unsung with your great idea.

The Clean and Unclean Animal

For you a man or woman in the market place of life, both the clean and the unclean animals are of significance in your social capital build up. People talk of social capital today, but it's not a new concept at all. God told Noah to take all kinds of creature into the ark. He didn't only take the ones he liked; he took the ones that are needed. He didn't take just the clean ones; he also took the unclean ones. The unclean ones have their own use as well in the larger picture. Some of them may be too unclean for consumption but not too unclean to make manure for Noah's farm. He truly had seven pairs of the clean ones each and two pairs of the unclean ones. This means while you are building your social capital, your assets must outweigh your liabilities in relationship building. Some people are outright assets, make more of such, some are more of liabilities, you need to keep some of them as well.

The issue with your relationships or social capital is that it has the ability to open doors for you to find use and profiting for your other forms of capital. If you don't value or pay attention to such relationships, such doors may not open. For you in market place of life, all the three levels of relationships will work for you and add to your capital pool.

i. **The Capital of Upward Relationship:** Parents, teachers, coaches, mentors, bosses, employers and authorities fall under this category. Any of these can open doors for you with ease if they find you worthy of their investing upon. Most of the times, they will open doors for you by choice for your own good as benevolence or service to humanity. They see helping you as an investment into goodwill. It takes humility, serving upward and favour to really come under such benevolence apart from blood relationship.

Your capital for lifetime breakthrough in enterprise might be a single recommendation from someone higher. Even when you know that you have something higher in stock, you need to humble yourself for this leverage first. Do not be too big and cocky in your own eye; do not have entitlement attitude either. Reap the capital of upward relationship by recognising the natural law of respect, order and hierarchy.

Nobody really cares to know the name and what became of Pharaoh after the famine. But as for Joseph, histories have been written and re-written in books, songs and movies. Joseph realised the value of such social capital and made most of it through humility. Joseph stood before Pharaoh, and not the other way round; even though he was the one who had the solution to the national problem at that time.

ii. ***The Capital of Horizontal Relationship:*** Mates and colleagues are value adding as far as you are concerned. There is a common term of being a team player we often use in modern day to make the resume look good. Beyond resume packaging, being able to work well in a team is a crucial capital that can determine your destiny. I saw a documentary on the selection of the famed 'Dream Team' of the American basketball that won the Olympic gold medal in 1992 at Barcelona. That team was reputed to be the best team ever assembled in the game. Need I to say that the success of that team greatly enriched the career profile and memories of everyone privileged to be in the team in no small measure. I read some of them saying that was the best career memory and achievement they ever had. Of note in the selection process was the decision of the coaching crew to drop even obviously good and hugely talented players as long as they would not be team players. Team players, not only on court but off it. You can truly be better and more loaded in other forms of capital, including skills than everyone else and yet you may come out a failure in the market simply because of relationship failure. Your gifting could truly be a major part of the puzzle, but a major part is still only a part. The beauty and meaning of the puzzle only comes out when you are joined to the other parts no matter how minor they seem.

> Your gifting could truly be a major part of the puzzle, but a major part is still only a part.

When the people you spend most of your time with outside your blood family have nothing to contribute to your career and enterprise dream, you are wasting your social capital of relationship. Making friends outside your purpose is recreation and if recreation dominates your time and use of energy, you are not a good handler of life resources. Many mates and friends so called are capital depleting. The sooner you move away from them the quicker you will build up something tangible for your personal advancement.

iii. ***The Capital of Downward Relationship:*** This includes relationship with employees, mentees, apprentices and such likes. As long as they have an input into what you are doing, they can make it work well or ruin it for you. They help you save cost or make you spend more than necessary. The worth of your staff's loyalty in the overall capital value of your enterprise cannot be over emphasised. Many companies keep pulling crowd of clients not just because of the quality of their goods or services but also the attitude of their staff. Happy staff will make your clients (customers) happy in general. They can take it out on your client if you are a jerk as boss. It is easy to know how good the boss has been by observing the average enthusiasm and the staff's willingness to go the extra mile across board.

We live in human world where you will need human relationship by every means and at all cost to bring value into your life investments as capital. Good relationship with a client in service or good delivery can leverage an organisation into success than a million dollar advertisements, much more in this hyper-sensitive generation of social media. Same goes for good relationships with colleagues and partners or even bosses.

CHAPTER

THE TANGIBLE CAPITAL OF SKILL

Farming requires skills and Noah required these skills no matter how blessed he was. We live in a world skillfully crafted by the creator himself. All creations in plants, animals and humans are well sculptured with unquestionable skills of God. We cannot afford to be skill-less in a world crafted with skill. Our relevance on earth and our skills are so connected that our ultimate capital value in the market depends largely on the connection.

> And Noah began to be a farmer, and he planted a vineyard.
> Genesis 9:20

What Noah chose or even determined to be was not what

ultimately determined his success, but what he 'did'. Noah planted a vineyard. He exhibited plant husbandry skills and reaped grapes out of which he also made wine.

Grace and favours are not substitutes for requisite skills. I am a Pastor and I pray for people to be favoured in the market place of life because I believe in favour and we often have great testimonies along that line in our assembly. Let us imagine a scenario of great miracle where I pray for a beloved member and he or she gets a job as a pilot even without flying skills. Imagine me travelling the day after he or she has just shared the testimony of such unprecedented favour only to find out that my well favoured member is the captain of the airplane I would be flying in. You of course know what would be my reaction and decision at the boarding gate no matter how important the trip could have been. Even me that anointed the person for favour will flee for my dear life with godly fear and trembling. This simple picture shows us the irreplaceable place of skill in successful enterprise building.

I remember growing up in the commercial city of Lagos, Nigeria, where almost everybody was always looking for money to 'do businesses. What they meant by business then were some kind of trading or contract execution without prior training or skill as long as 'capital' showed up. Capital in their context then was money. Many would see the money then and start off a so called business that would never fly but ultimately die off. Most of them would not sit down to acknowledge the absence of requisite skill for the business as the reason for their failure. They would rather blame the government, the environment, a witch or a wizard in the family.

It takes skill to showcase and bring together the value in the other forms of capital whether tangible or intangible for profiting enterprise building. Imagine a professional athlete with a great coach and team but no skill at all. Imagine a medical doctor with no medical skill, just certificate and more certificates. The reality of the market today is that employers are interested in what you can do than the number of degrees you have acquired.

Skill based professional certification started giving masters and doctoral degrees a very good run in the employment market this day for obvious reason. Who you are can be important, but what you can do really matters more today. I am not advocating abandoning your pursuit of formal education and degrees by any means, but we still need to reckon with the fact that many people abandoned their pursuit of university degrees to focus on honing their skills and they came up with astounding success. Note that they didn't abandon their university education to go drinking or as a result of laziness or purposeless pursuit. They did to focus on the ingenuity in them by the way of skill development and dispatch.

Skill Capital from Talent and Gifts

Some people are endowed with special abilities ranging from entertaining, sporting and several other talents and gifts. No matter how talented or gifted you are, to create capital value out of them you need to hone those talents and gifts in skills in some area of relevance.

Therefore, skill can be gotten from talent or gift subjected to development through rigorous training and discipline to generate maximum value therein. Many of us had some sporting gifts at one point or the other as we were growing up; but only those who honed theirs to skill level are the ones who get paid in millions for that same gift or talent today. Skillfulness at the global stage level where it becomes a trading platform for the skilled is

> "Skill can be gotten from talent or gift subjected to development through rigorous training and discipline to generate maximum value therein."

not just a mere matter of luck, being gifted or simply talented. Michael Phelps is said to be gifted with a swimmer's body including his trunk, feet, arms and palms. But those gifts still would never translate to Olympic gold medal without developing them to winning skill. Many people were born and bred on water like fish and had swam all their days but can never win any Olympic medal talk less of gold. I read of Phelps' training regime and build-up towards the 2008 Olympic in China. He was said to have trained for several hours literally everyday a year before that Olympic except for two days which were when he had a root canal treatment done on his tooth and the New year Day. He is the most decorated Olympian today by miles with over twenty medals, eighteen of which are gold. But he trained on his good days, his bad days and even his birthdays. You cannot be lucky than you have been brought close to luck by many deliberate factors including your skills. No matter how lucky I am, I cannot win the 100 Metre Olympic gold medal in 2016 at Rio, Brazil. I would not even be admitted close to where the luck can happen by the organisers of the race. This is simply because I lack the requisite build up for skill needed for such 'luck'.

Skill determines the ease with which you will do what others struggle to do. Everybody can possibly kick a football, but those who kick it past their opponent with ease and guide it skillful till it goes into a narrow space called the goal post are called the professionals. They get watched, idolised and paid ridiculous amount for the skills they display in the manner and ease of doing it. Teams from serious leagues travel across the world to scout for talented and gifted players and turn them to skillful players through rigorous training and refining. After a while, these same players are light years in skills and achievement ahead of their childhood playmates of possibly same gifts and talents who lack their kind of discipline and training experiences. When you are ready to go through the refining fire of discipline and training with your gifts and talents, you surely will come out on the other side with value generating capital of skill.

When you are ready to go through the refining fire of discipline and training with your gifts and talents, you surely will come out on the other side with value generating capital of skill.

Skill Capital Acquired

Skills can also be built on a platform that never existed before. I mean you can acquire skill without any prior gift or talent along that line. Necessity and interest can give birth to skill acquisition for you. We had a teaching on how blessing works in our Church one time and a young man heard it and acted on it. He saw the need to acquire some relevant skills in a field, far away from his original profession, in order to boost his capital in the market place of life. He started on the internet with self-training and later went for few courses along that line. He got a job from an interview with the preliminary skill he acquired from self-training on the internet. He made some money and then started acquiring more skills from trainings on job and in more training. Today he is at par and even better employed in that field than many who had their primary degree in that same field. He had his first and master degrees in an extremely far away field, but he saw the necessity and developed the interest to be trained.

With minimal pressure, anyone can cut through human flesh with surgical scalpel even if with a gasp. But the surgeon is skilled in cutting with ease till he removes the diseased part of the body and put the patient back in better form. They are revered, employed, paid and given licence to cut based on the presence of these skills, whether you are white or black, male or female. Skill acquisition therefore is capital accumulation. If

If you can do it, we will all standby and give you way to help us out.

you can do it, we will all standby and give you way to help us out. We will pay you at the end and also say 'thank you'. Every endeavour in life that attracts rewards requires skill. Nobody gets paid for eating and drinking naturally because those require no skill. But if by any chance you are a connoisseur; eating and drinking comes with skills for you but also with payment.

In a nutshell, skill is:

1.   Being able to do the task efficiently.
2.   Being able to do the task efficiently well.
3.   Being able to do the task efficiently well with ease.
4.   Being able to do the task efficiently well with ease in the most excellent way.
5.   Being able to do the task efficiently well with ease in the most excellent way within reasonable time.
6.   Being able to do the task efficiently well with ease in the most excellent way within reasonable time with the least possible complication.
7.   *Skill therefore, means ability gradient to deliver which can always be improved upon.*

This seventh description of skill brings us to the concept of competence. Because of the presence of gradient, quality range is therefore a must in our consideration.

Competence Is Value

The capital value in skill is mostly competence dependent. From zero to zenith is the gradient of skill in its various forms. The capital value of your skill depends on where it falls in the gradient of capacity for delivery. This brings us to the issue of incompetence which means the absence of requisite skill for delivery. Beyond mere absence of requisite skill, incompetence can be an absence of the skill to know the limit of your skill. Competence shows you the difference between when to deliver, when to defer and when to refer. Competence

> "Competence shows you the difference between when to deliver, when to defer and when to refer."

at its height in every profession takes speciality into consideration. No skill confers a know-it-all or do-it-all capacity on anyone. Part of your competence in skilfulness is to let others do it when they can do it better.

Capacity Development

Skill is never in-born. Talents and gifts as we have seen earlier can be providence given but skills are only made out of them through rigorous training, discipline and exercise. This is one major reason for failures in leadership in many third World countries where leadership selection is froth in sentiments than competence. Many consider themselves as born leaders, but there is nothing as such.

Capacity to deliver good leadership is a function of leadership skill development. Formal education will help but will not get the job done totally. So we see many Harvard trained and Oxford trained leaders who are everything but competent. They have read the concepts of leadership in books but they are not subject to the rigorous discipline therein and so are unskillful at leadership. The downward movement of their places of leadership in every index of development bear testimonies loud and clear to their incompetence and capacity deficiencies in leadership.

You can inherit an organisation, a position or an enterprise by birth, but the level of your competence to take the enterprise forward is not in-born. You need to acquire and keep upgrading it through rigorous capacity development. Capacity development in leadership and other skills have to do with the following:

• Rigorous training in relevant skills acquisition.
• Requisite Discipline for requisite skills fine tuning.
• Exercise against being stuck in skill comfort zone.
• Personal application of known truth.

• Continuous education for skill upgrade based on evolving needs of the day.

Irreplaceable Place of Skill
1.   Skill Confers Boldness:
Skill is akin to wisdom; it gives you the boldness of approach to the task at hand. When you know what to do, how to do and when to do with certainty and dexterity, your approach is void of ultimate fidgeting even if you had the initial butterfly of taking off. The way a skillful surgeon approaches tissue cutting no matter how gory looking with certainty of saving the patient at the end is what skill is about. He is certain of what to cut, what to crush and what to spare. Even when it looks like he is killing the patient in the eye of an unskilled observer, he knows that he is on the right path of approach.

> Who is as the wise man? and who knoweth the interpretation of a thing? a man's wisdom maketh his face to shine, and the boldness of his face shall be changed. Ecclesiastes 8:1

2.   Skill Brings Ease:
A skillful pilot approaches flying with so much ease even when every other person on board is tensed up for a reason or the other. Skills acquired by training, practice and experience over the years of flying under all kinds of weather take away tension and panic or else he/she will

die of panic attack in not so long. What you are well skilled for does not wear you out easily.

3.   *Skill Saves Time:*

When you are skillful in a field, you will not only know the surest and safest route to the desired goal. You will also know the shortest path along that sure and safe route. What an untrained person will use eternity to explain to someone with hearing impairments will be communicated with ease and in a matter of seconds by another person who is well skilled in sign language.

> **The labour of fools wearies them, for they do not even know how to go to the city.**
> **Ecclesiastes 10 :15**

4.   *Skill Saves Cost:*

The undesirable costs of having leaders who are only skilled in being enthroned and not in the art of leading show in nations of the world all over whenever enthronement is manipulated by ballot or baton. Unskillful workers cost their enterprise a lot in money, time and reputation. Some can even cost innocent lives. Skill saves us the unintended and unnecessary cost in our endeavour.

> **If the iron be blunt, and he do not whet the edge then must he put to more strength: but wisdom is profitable to direct.**
> **Ecclesiastes 10:10**

Strength cost in the context of

above is the cost of not being skillful enough to know when to sharpen up the instrument in use. When you have respect for skill and cost, you will crave improvement at every point along the way.

5.   *Skill Allows for Standardisation:*
Excellence and safety can only be guaranteed when there are standards to follow by all and sundry. Many field in human endeavour that require high quality of delivery are saddled with rigorous training of their professional until they acquire a level of skill deemed as the threshold for practitioners in such fields. One of the reason for failure in political leadership across the world is because there are no specific skill requirements and thus the blur line of standardisation. Anybody can aspire for position and become the custodian of multitude destinies with little or no skill in attending to issues that are sacrosanct to their well-being. Skill separates the professionals from quacks in fields where skills are the requisite for being a practitioner. They are guided, guarded, regulated, promoted and called to question based on the skill standard expected of them. This probably tells us why many quacks are there in political offices, business and ministries across the globe causing havocs and depleting values in the field.

6.   *Skill Allows for Transition:*

Because human days on earth are numbered, much more their active days in enterprise; transitions become inevitable. Passing the baton to the next generation without compromising the standard must be a great concern in every human endeavour. This brings us back to the concept of standard and the skills necessary to attain such. There is always smooth generational transition in certain profession because the skills required are outlined and passed on by the penultimate generation. Skill does not allow enterprise to die with people. There are always people with requisite skill to keep it going.

7.   *Skill gives Room for Better:*

Because of the tangibility of skill, improvement is much possible. Skill is one capital that can easily be improved to improve productivity. Skills can be adopted, adapted, dropped or improved upon. Better ways of doing things can be researched, perfected and established as standard. We live in a dynamic world and so does skill allow for dynamism.

CHAPTER 9

THE TANGIBLE CAPITAL OF MATERIAL SUBSTANCE (MONEY CAPITAL)

Noah planted seeds of grapes bearing vines. Material capital can be money or goods. It could be land, landed property or equipment. Noah had respect for his material goods and so invested them in the soil for a return in harvest. He could have eaten all the seeds he came out of the ark with. He could have allowed them to rot away somewhere because they probably were not many. Most of the resources we waste on gratification could have served the purpose of capital in our hand if we value them and not throw them away.

Money Habits

Material capital mostly is a product of our money habit. Whereas many are sitting down and hoping to pick up a bag full of millions one day along the highway by providence, some wise folks have already seen providence in the little they have and are planning to turn it over till it becomes the bag full of millions in their hands. Money becomes capital in your hand when you develop a healthy and balanced habit of handling it. Money you use in self-development is money invested and spent wisely. Your attitude with money can bring favour or make enemy for you.

Making money is important but handling it is more important for a man or woman who wants to build a successful enterprise. Being stingy and being wasteful will not do; holding money in the right perspective as a tool to be used and also to be kept will do.

> Money becomes capital in your hand when you develop a healthy and balanced habit of handling it.

Money as capital is not just as a start-up for your enterprise but it is important as a backup for it ultimately. To be able to gather money is not as important as to what you do with what you gather. Making money will definitely increase the credit rating of your enterprise and make available unto you the money you have not yet earned in various credit forms and facilities. Credit cards, overdrafts, loans and other credit facilities are useful and can give you some capital leverage. They can also be tempting and deceptive as well. Do not be trapped into overestimating your enterprise material worth, thereby prompting spending spree into financial toxicity.

The Capital in Little

The objective of this book is not for it to be a be-it-all and cure-it-all wisdom base for building a successful enterprise as no singular book can ever be that, no matter how versatile and deep the author is. The essence of this book is to narrow it down to specific cases that are applicable to you as a reader and make you see the wisdom therein. This is why we are looking at the concept of enterprise with the man Noah in focus.

Consider the scenario where Noah found himself, God told Noah to take human and animals but not plant. God told him to take food but not seed for farming. It was Noah's prerogative that prompted him to make seed out of whatever fruits were left in their storage at the point of disembarking the ship. The foods were probably well spent at this point and it just finished flooding, so Noah had excuses to continue sitting, eating and waiting till the conditions become conducive.

Here was Noah making capital of the little remaining to kick start his idea. The major issue with capital is that it is like human fingers that are not equal in length ever. You may not have the luxury of starting big like someone else. A little start can be the good start you need. The goods hoarded in the sheds and lofts can be your capital wasting away. The car parked outside may be the capital you have been looking for all this while. There perhaps will not be a time where you will be able to lay hold of such huge amount you are dreaming about to start with in the nearest now. This may necessitate a change of strategy for you, which can include a change of venture.

Breakthrough in a small venture may be your open door unto the big venture you have always been dreaming of. Little money can be used to acquire big capital. Think of the little money in your hand being used for skill acquisition or bridge building in social capital. The little may not be big enough to qualify for capital in itself; but can open doors for you into other or bigger capital if well utilised.

Comfort or Capital

> Don't build your house and establish a home until your fields are ready, and you are sure that you can earn a living.
> Proverbs 24:27 (GNT)

The heart of the matter in this passage is that certain comfort can wait for now. What looks good for consumption can be your capital, don't eat it up. Certain trend of fashion, certain holiday trips and many more comforts can be capital going down the drain of pleasure unknown. Building an enterprise requires the discipline of delayed gratification. Noah had a choice of eating the grapes there and then or planting it to own a whole vineyard with wine press later.

There are certain neighbourhoods you don't have any business living in for now; the best you can do is to have your occasional walk around the area to catch inspiration and then go back home to work hard till your size changes. There are certain cars you must not drive at some phase of your life or else you want to remain a struggler. There are certain kind of private schools and costly recreations for children you should not be spending so exorbitantly on now. Otherwise you will remain in the struggle of creating false image of comfort class, with the huge price of capital depletion and true great discomfort behind the scene. With the lopsided emphasis on packaging in this age, you need to know that your enterprise capacity to execute projects is far dependent on its material capital base than on image and appearance. Your material capital size has nothing much, if any at all, to do with the glamour of your packaging. Material capacity is a stark reality that stares you right in the eyes when the need to deliver arises. Do not shy away from it; just be true to yourself and build up ahead. Serious and successful enterprise builders are concerned about capital build-up rather than comfort and image pile-up.

Salient points to consider:

- Skill creates the ultimate capital of relevance.
- Skill is only as valuable as the cost of honing it.
- The ultimate links between you and where you are going are human; pay attention to relationship.
- Perspective that birth proper handling is what makes capital out of material possession, including money.
- Capital development and management requires rigorous exercise and discipline.

10

ENTERPRISE OBJECTIVE OF DISCOVERING MISSING LINK

NOAH'S ENTERPRISE OBJECTIVE

Measurable progress or falling short of the target can only be better appreciated when a goal is aimed at before effort is applied to any endeavour in life. Whether as a person or as an organisation, knowing well that you are a mere part of the larger global picture is important. This will help you define your field of activities, your kind of activities, the scope of your activities and the expected impacts or results from your activities. Your enterprise objective simply answers the specific question of 'why are you in the market place'. Your answer cannot just be 'to succeed or 'to make money'.

Because success is relative in various ramifications, an athlete who represents his or her country in the Olympic without winning a medal can see it as success and truly it is, depending on the athlete's career objective in doing the sport. To be selected to represent your country in the first place means you are the best among your equal at the national level, which is success. Waving one's country flag at the opening ceremony of the Olympic before the whole World is a ramification of success. Having your country's flag raised above your head with the national anthem blaring and gold medal glittering on your neck simultaneously is also success, surely at another level. Neither of these are mere event of happenstance. They are all and various products of career objectives set out by an athlete and backed up with corresponding pursuit to match.

Your enterprise objective simply answers the specific question of 'why are you in the market place'.

Noah knew what he was doing so much that he even knew what to do with his bountiful harvest. He didn't just harvest grapes from his vine for harvest sake; he made wine out of same. His goals were set out clear and crisp once he saw the situation on the ground after the flood. He wanted to be a farmer, but not just a plant harvesting farmer. He wanted to be a wine brewing farmer.

When your enterprise objectives are clearly spelt out and are given the right kind of pursuit, success and money will come as part of the rewards. You will stay at the competitive edge of the market. In fact, you will be at the forefront while others will be competing with you. Noah had three enterprise objectives we can see clearly from his account:

1. Enterprise Objective of Discovering Missing Idea

The man Noah saw that plant had been swept away by flood and mankind will need fruits ere the one in storage finished. Possibly the animals were reproducing in the ark and so increasing but it had not been so for the plants. Everything we call development today in our world is a product of idea. God didn't create development; God only put development in man as ability to bring forth and pursue idea and improve on same

That idea rules the world is an age long truth and will remain so for ever. Whatever we are enjoying today in goods or services were crystallised out of someone's or a group's idea.

> "God didn't create development; God only put development in man as ability to bring forth and pursue idea and improve on same."

You get rewarded with value in their various forms, sizes and at various levels when you invest value into solving problem. Let us take a case study of *'hunger and appetite problem'* being solved by a restaurant. There are chefs, waiters, cleaners, store keepers, securities, accountants and many more. All of them are doing different things under different roles with different skills to the end that clients might come in and have good food in a good and secure environment. They will be rewarded in various forms including salaries with career development as workers. There will be profits for the owner(s) with reputations amongst many for the brand itself. This picture is value creating or value adding in various forms and at various levels, bringing about rewards in various measure to those who are engaged therein.

The tendency to start thinking some weird unrealisable stuff in your head, having heard about idea, is high. But to help you I will narrow it down to few sub-headings below based on the above simple scenario.

(i)   *Human Needs Are Definite and Obvious*
We live in human world; every other creation is here because of humanity including the animals we raise as pets or those in wild. They are called pets because someone is keeping them as such. As vast as human

needs seem, they are simple and definite. All human productivities for ages with the attendant infinite zillion monetary investments revolve around specific needs. Human needs are either basic primary needs for survival and security or the higher secondary needs for expression and recreation. We want to express our individuality, ingenuity, tastes, desires, dominions and many more. Abraham Maslow did a fair job in categorising human needs in their order of importance in what is known today as Maslow's hierarchy of need.4.1. Whether the need is basic or higher, it will take some idea crystallised into some goods or services to meet it.

When someone is concerned about human needs which includes the needs of what man is interested in such as animal, ideas can be conceived to solve them. Primarily, a restaurant solves hunger and appetite problem; any other peck that comes with it is an addition. The concern might be self-serving as it were, in which case people pay and you make the profit, but the issue is the concern to meet their needs being there first.

One of the major reason Christians seem not to be dominating the market place of whatever nation they find themselves, in-spite of all the grace, faith and blessing they carry, is the lack of concern for human needs. We love to play God, it's just that we don't play it well because even God the Almighty recognised and acknowledged human needs. We tend to be so caught up in our own world that we just abandon the earth and its attending human needs to the unsaved. The reality is that as long as heaven has not happened, we will live here on earth and be faced with the reality of human needs. Whosoever meets the needs will be rewarded with wealth and dominion that comes with relevance as far as the earth is concerned.

God knew the tendency for His people to live in a bubble when he inspired Jeremiah to instruct them ahead of their being carried away to Babylon in captivity for seventy years. Seventy years is long that you cannot just be living like you will leave tomorrow. I will not be tempted to go into the theology behind the prophecy. But note that the verse we will look at is the build up to the famed *'thoughts of good and not evil'* in *Jeremiah 29:11*. In fact God warned his people not to listen to sanctimonious prophets who would want to teach them to close their eyes to the reality of the needs in their land of captivity. He knew that religious leaders would want to deceive them into hiding the heads in the sand and live in denial of the obvious needs of the day. Hear what God said in prophecy:

God was simply saying, be concerned with definitive actions for the needs of where you are, which is the earth in a broader sense now, then your needs on the earth will be met. There are no Christian foods or Christians clothes in the stores;

> And seek the peace of the city whither I have caused you to be carried away captives, and pray unto the LORD for it: for in the peace thereof shall ye have peace.
> Jeremiah 29:7.

there is no exclusive Christian house or transportation. When it comes to human needs, universality applies to a great extent. Your rewards and relevance goes a long way in you standing to be counted in meeting any or some of them. Ideas come when you are concerned about human needs to the end that you may contribute your own quota no matter how little in meeting them.

> "Ideas come when you are concerned about human needs to the end that you may contribute your own quota no matter how little in meeting them."

(ii) Human Needs Are Elastic

The reason behind the setting up of our restaurant above might not just be inspired by the desire to meet hunger and appetite needs. It could be location-inspired in other to meet the needs of certain demography. It could be to serve certain kind of tastes in a particular manner. The setting of the famed McDonald's was not just to serve potato chips and chicken or beef burger which forms the basic course of their meals in any case. It was more of the manner it is being served than what is being served.

There are various fashion houses with various styles and signatures all over the world today and many more will still come in the future. They all are tapping into the elasticity of style and taste in the basic human need to be covered in clothing.

The need for mobile means of communication in telephoning was pioneered by Motorola and Ericsson with breakthrough in the early sixties. The basic use of mobile phone is communication for ever, but the elasticity associated with human need for same has evolved in leaps and bounds over time. Some could see through this and came up with what we call smart phones today. Much more than smart phones in mobile telecommunications are still on the way and they will generate their own markets and values on arrival. *Human needs evolve; they are elastic and have infinite capacity to stretch within the confines of the definite. It takes an observing heart to see them and innovate ideas for meeting them.*

When Solomon said nothing is new under the heaven, he was not talking in the context of innovations. If you innovate ideas in goods or services to meet the ever evolving needs of man, you will be rewarded with success and wealth. Everything keeps evolving, including basic things such as domestic needs, forever.

(iii) Human Needs Can Be Latent

As definite, basic and obvious as human needs are, the concept of evolution of needs with the context of elasticity of the same means that obvious will not always be the case. Human needs may have to be dug out by ideas. Human needs can be lying dormant or hidden for ages, waiting for someone to come and stir it up with ideas.

The idea of working with typewriter may be so strange to an average worker today in the University I graduated from in about two decades ago. But in just over two decades ago when I was admitted into the same university, every office was powered by typists and secretaries sitting behind typewriters. In fact, as near as 1992 the whole college of Medicine then had only one computer and it was in the Provost's office. This computer could only be operated by about two people. I remember this because it took them an extra day to release our Pre-

Clinic 1 examination results. Contrary to the tradition of releasing the results the same day the examiners met, it took them an extra day or two because someone was entering the result into the computer in the Provost's office. It was like someone went to the moon to accomplish it. My first book was written in 1994 while I was a student in the same institution with the typesetting done with a typewriter. When I see how everything is paralysed in offices today if the internet goes down, I always wonder how we used to cope before the mid-nineties release of worldwide web. Nobody was complaining then and life went on just fine across the world. But some innovative ideas have stirred up our latent needs and appetite; now we cannot do without computer or internet and their allied gadgets in our personal spaces and offices.

There are still zillions of dormant needs that humanity will only acknowledge when someone comes up with the solution by innovative ideas. Can you imagine how they used to cope in the world when there were no cars or air planes? The basic need of movement was being met then, but hidden in humanity as latent within that basic need for movement was the elastic need of flying, flying far and flying fast in airplane. The Wright brothers could not imagine what aviation has metamorphosed into today, even though they saw the need for flying.

The world is for those who will dig deep and think far to reach the depth of creativity for what is missing. From my observation, it is easier to pray and fast than to think. I do take my two children to the office and spare us the minder's fee whenever the school is on break. The days I am just fasting and praying in the office are easier for me in this Daddy's day-care task. Whenever I want to think, plan or write; I find them so distracting and I find myself on edge, less productive and frustrated.

It is compulsory to pray and fast, but it is more compulsory to download what heaven has deposited in me while praying. This can only be done through deep thinking and meditation with rapt attention. Many of us are missing out on what heaven has prepared for those who love God, which is who we are, not because heaven is not transferring the data but simply because we are not downloading them.

There are always missing ideas in every age and generation; those who go for and discover them put themselves on higher platform of productivity. Noah did and started planting grapes and making wine. Whether they are obvious, latent or evolving, human needs are real and will always form the basis of the world's economic growth and development. You can take your own slice of the cake by setting out a simple objective of going for the missing ideas.

More than Discoveries and Conception

Having discussed the concept of missing idea extensively as a major enterprise objective for Noah after the flood; we need to see the other two sides of Noah's empire building objectives. My fear is for someone to read this book and start having some lofty ideas that have no head or tail or delivery system and point. As a public speaker, I have seen people hear stirring oration and taking impulsive steps accordingly but with no mapped out actions that will see the steps crystallised into concrete desired results.

CHAPTER 11

ENTERPRISE OBJECTIVE OF BUILDING THE MISSING LINK

This is Noah's second enterprise objective. Of what use is an idea of a purported human need that has no real relevance to the so called human except in the head of the one conceiving the idea. Noah's idea was not weird and so lofty that it had no link to the reality of his time. His second business objective was to be able to link the so called missing idea to that reality. He was set to conceptualise the delivery system for his idea. Let's set up a farm. A farm will link the seed, the ground and the nutrient together, hurray!

Have you come across people whose business and career

ideas can only be executed in the galaxies among aliens? How grandeur your idea is, so called, is not what will make it deliver success. Your idea will succeed if it has realistic relevance to human need such that you can easily work out a delivery system. Do not just find an idea; conceptualise it in a very simple and user friendly way. Humans by nature do not like strenuous task if they are paying already. If it is not simply linked, it is wrongly conceptualised, even though rightly conceived.

> "If it is not simply linked, it is wrongly conceptualised, even though rightly conceived."

Noah could have been thinking of 'on-the-sea' projects, seeing he was surrounded by water, but he rather went for the simple one on ground. Noah had some seeds, he definitely had animal manure, and some dry ground. He was able to link his farming idea to the present realities. Many seeds of idea have floated away because they were sown on the sea. If Martin Luther King Jnr. had embarked on arms struggle in realising 'the dream' he had, he probably wouldn't have lived long to even deliver the speech he is known with today. I have seen young men in developing nations of Africa conceiving ideas of freedom from repressive and oppressive leaders discuss their lofty ideas. What is always lacking across board is the delivery system. Some who are ignorant will even quickly call for revolution in term of war and arm struggle. Conceiving an idea is a great side of a good coin, but it is not yet a legal tender until you come up with the better side of workable delivery system.

Bridge for Efficiency

When talking of efficiency, a bridge for crossing a river comes to mind easily. It saves time and saves us of possible loss. The bridge is just a simple link between two points and same goes for the concept of building missing links in the market place of ideas. A doctor is a bridge between the patient and hospital. The hospital has an idea of making health service delivery available to the patient but several professional bodies come up with links to build an efficient delivery system to that effect. When building efficient and improving already existent bridges between ideas and needs are set in focus, relevance that gives room for success will always avail itself to you or your organisation.

This point brings us to the place of realising that your idea might just be a small compliment bringing the missing link to already existing ideas. Having a great idea does not mean you must start something new and different; your value may be better delivered though an existing system.

The boom in oil and gas demand and supply towards the beginning of twentieth century led to the springing of many allied industries that created great wealth for many involved therein. In the same vein, the boom we are experiencing in the Information Technology today has led to the huge surge in value generation and wealth creations through many IT-related fields and allied companies. Many are just serving as link builders between the main services and goods providers. Some serve as links between the goods or services providers and their mammoth end users.

Grape was not introduced to the then world by Noah; so the idea was necessary not originally his own. Probably grapes had been growing naturally here and there before then. Probably wine makers before the flood had always had the raw materials challenge dwarfing the industry. When Noah disembarked the ark, one of his enterprise objectives was to build the missing link between the winery and vineyards. He succeeded in doing so and was the first to be recorded as doing so.

Dear reader, your enterprise objective may not be to discover ideas; it may be to build the missing links of delivery systems between already discovered and existent ideas. The global enterprise as a whole is a worldwide web of dependency and inter-dependence of sort. You will be solving humongous problems also by simply being the missing links among existent ideas.

When it comes to ideas, you will be surprised that loads of people have them in abundance and in various forms here and there in their heads. The ones who succeed nevertheless in the school of idea are the ones who are able to string them together in order to create a framework of pursuit; a feasible delivery system. Capacity to not only conceive but to conceptualise ideas into a simple framework of action points or pursuit was Noah's strong point. While an idea is a question of 'what', *seeing the missing link is 'how'*. Noah knew that his household and the world needed fruits, so he began to meet the need in becoming a farmer. He had the *'what' and knew the 'how'* in the most effective way. You need to see the 'what' and know the 'how' too.

CHAPTER 12

ENTERPRISE OBJECTIVE OF FILLING THE VOIDS

Noah was not just thinking of an idea; neither was he just conceptualising them; *he was doing them*. Delivery point is the rewarding point for ideas. If you don't deliver your idea at the point of need, someone else will and gets rewarded for it. The world is less interested in who invented or innovated or first came up with what as an idea; they are more interested in who delivers what at the point of need. One of your major enterprise objectives is to deliver at the point of need. Whether it is a service or sub-service; whether it is a good or sub-good.

Talk is cheap; only doers are rewarded with enterprise

success. Even for those whose profession is to talk, talking has become a doing for them. One of my pains is seeing people talking of how they too had the same idea after another person has delivered it and they see that person being rewarded with success in kind, cash and otherwise for delivering the idea. You are rewarded when the void is filled, not when you talk about or see the void. Noah probably sat down to learn being a farmer but *'learning' and 'being' it is not as important as 'doing' it.* Serious employers want excellent delivery on the job, not qualifications.

Excellent Delivery, Good Patronage
As long as you fill the voids well, you will be patronised. Why is it that some service providers get more than enough clients while others are struggling to get by? The answer might be in filling the voids. The name, the brand and the logo are not as important as the ability to fill the void excellently.

About two decades ago, there was a rumour about the CEO/Chairman of a major US based global organisation being anti-Christian and being a Satanist. The rumour was so rife and targeted at turning the mammoth Christian population, especially in Africa, away from using the company's product. One of their products then was the most popular baby nappy product where I lived. After all was said and done, the product still dominated the market and kept selling very well. Sentiments and emotional blackmail could not turn multitude of Christians away from the product. This was simply because the product perfectly filled the void. It was the best in market then. A user's choice is guided by what fills the void of excellent quality and competitive cost first before any other perennial consideration.

> "A user's choice is guided by what fills the void of excellent quality and competitive cost first before any other perennial consideration."

I am a practising Christian but will not ask if a product was manufactured by an atheist or someone with other religious affiliations before purchasing it if it fills the void for what I need it. This is where excellence comes in. *Excellence includes delivering the goods or services at the most competitive cost in the most convenient way within the best time frame conceivable, where it's needed and when it's needed.* It is easy to know how unbelievers dominate markets, when every beautiful and excellent product is manufactured by marine spirit, in the heads of believers. If it is not marine spirit, it will be illuminati. Such a mediocre thinking is a total ostrich approach to the issue of excellent delivery in goods and services.

Noah delivered; you need to, and excellently for that matter. It must be your enterprise objective. I will rather employ an excellent sinner than a mediocre saint when it comes to certain goods and services delivery. Noah was the first consumer of his product and so the need to do it well. First put yourself in the position of the consumer of your goods or services and then bring out the excellence in you for satisfaction.

"First put yourself in the position of the consumer of your goods or services and then bring out the excellence in you for satisfaction."

Don't Rob Us

These three enterprise objective became the bedrock and launching pad upon which Noah's enterprise was built. Talking about followership, Noah had a good template to follow here. Before running to the market place of life, ask yourself the salient question of objective. Do not just go 'to be successful' or 'make money' so to say; go with the value driven objectives enumerated above and you will stay at the cutting edge of relevance in the market. You will make money and have success but with traceable impact on your field of trade.

It is not a good testimony when people show us their bling and tell us of their mountain of cash and yet we cannot see the impacts of the goods or services that have been delivered. It could be entertainment, it could be sports, it could be faith enterprise or any good or service delivery and at whatever level. It could be sole enterprise or a part of larger enterprise, big or small, as explained before. When we cannot see the trace of their impact in meeting any legitimate market need, it is ripping and not reaping. I am not talking of charitable donations here; it is about how you made the money you are donating. Telling humanity how much you have made from her without her seeing how much she has gained from you in exchange for the value you gained is the simple definition of robbery. Coca Cola gave us a taste and some satisfaction in exchange for our money in their vaults all over the world. Apple gave us a minimalist approach to mobile gadgets. Microsoft gave us Windows. These are mega and the obvious but the list goes on endlessly in goods and services from micro to mega ones. The cleaner that creates the impact of a tidy environment. The counsellor who brought light into dilemma and confusion. The nurse who just took the blood pressure. They are all creating values and making impact in exchange for rewards in their

> "Telling humanity how much you have made from her without her seeing how much she has gained from you in exchange for the value you gained is the simple definition of robbery."

various enterprises. Whatever they gave us was the manifestation of their enterprise objectives or a reviewed fashion of same along the way.

Some salient points to consider:

- The value of an idea is in its delivery not mere conception.
- Human need are definite and yet elastic, obvious and yet latent; idea meets them all.
- The elasticity of human need within the confine of definite is infinite, therefore humanity cannot run out of veritable ideas bringing about profitable enterprises as long as the earth remains.
- Robbery is gaining value and reward, outside of welfare or charity, not in exchange for any valuable good or service delivery.
- Excellence comes when you put yourself at the receiving end of your goods or service delivery.

13

CHAPTER

NOAH'S
ENTERPRISE
IDEAL
OF DILIGENCE

Efficiency, excellence, continuous improvement and relevance are necessary for sustainable success in the market place. All of these virtues and many more are always ingrained in the value system of serious minded individual or organisation.

Enterprise ideal talks of standard that sets the boundaries and thresholds that everyone and every unit of operation within the enterprise cannot go beyond and fall short of. This becomes the striving standard, pace determinant and value setter for the enterprise.

Why Standard?

• *Standard is your driving force to be better and be best:* The problem with good is that it can occur by happenstance or mere desire not to settle for bad. But for better to follow good, someone will have to work against the inertia of complacency. You have to overlook good and strife more for a higher standard. The best comes when the strife for better continues without end because being the best is just a step further from better.

• *Standard solves the mystery of ability:* There is a mystery around human ability to deliver, which is that we human naturally deliver based on the push behind us. Whether the push from behind is a self-push from within, or motivated by an external factor such as the need to remain employed or the presence of competition; there has to be a push. This shows why athletes always run their best time in big competitions and when there are strong oppositions. Human brain loves rest than sweat; it takes serious challenges to bring out the best out of the human brain. Most of the profound inventions came out of challenges, whether internal or external. When there is enterprise ideal, everyone is shown where and

"Human brain loves rest than sweat; it takes serious challenges to bring out the best out of the human brain."

what to strive towards irrespective of what we perceive as our inherent abilities.

There was this story of a lovely lady in our church whom I challenged to arrive in church for service early and she just could not see why people will wake up that so early to come to church. For her, she didn't have the ability. Not long after then, her department at work was moved from London where she lives to another city. Her living with her family in the opposite edge of London meant she had to leave home some three hours to the time I asked her to be making it to Church by 9:30am in order for her to make it to work by 9:00am. She had done it for two weeks before I got to know and I asked her how she could cope with such 'unimaginable' schedule. Her answer was that 'she didn't even know herself that she could leave home that early even in her life'. She did that commuting for two to three months before God opened another door of work for her back in the city. The lesson there was that her company had its resumption hour standard every worker has to oblige with whether you feel you have ability to wake early or not.

• ***Standard solves the problem of generational shift***: This concept applies to individual and group enterprises. The shift in values and ideals across generations is too real to be denied. But the laws that guide life and living are still the same. For example, the law of gravity has passed through various generations and socio-cultural shifts in human history but it is still there. In order for you not to start playing dangerously in your enterprise pursuits because time has changed, you need to have ideals or standards that undergird your activities. Same goes for as many as will be involved now or in the future. They need standards to bring them to line against the backdrop of the unavoidable dangers in generational shift.

For example, the Information Technology revolution has created opportunities to work away from the office but the standard and value of diligence must be there to prevent people being rewarded for doing nothing.

Noah being the pioneer saint of the farmers is our standard in this book because the one before him was Cain but had no good ideal we can follow. Let us see Noah's ideal which is the standard every successful farmer subscribes to till date.

The Value of Diligence

Between seed and harvest is a big space called time. One of the major occupiers of that space called time is diligence. There is no food for the lazy man is a good saying whether the lazy man is a saint or a sinner. Diligence has no substitute in spirituality. God the Spirit himself was a diligent God. God worked six out of seven days and that should be the standard. He only rested one out of the seven days. When the order is reversed, the earth will remain empty dark and void. The easy way to ruin an enterprise till it is filled with darkness, emptiness and voids, either as an employee, partner or employer, is to overlook God's example of hard work and diligence. Hard work is not just expeditions of raw energy; hard work is being efficient and effective at the work for a large part of the time.

Noah did not just throw his seeds underground. He must have watched them coming out as blades, weeded round the vine, dealt with pests and nurtured the vine unto harvest. From planting, to nurturing and the harvest, the work type and load would have been different but had to be done.

Diligence therefore, is being where you ought to be, when you ought to be there and doing what you ought to be doing to the best of your abilities. Jesus had something to say while he was about to walk from one point to another as the work for that particular moment.

> Jesus answered, are there not twelve hours in the day?
> If anyone walks in the day, he does not stumble, because
> he sees the light of this world. But if one walks in the night,
> he stumbles, because the light is not in him.
> John 11:9-10.

Jesus' concept of walk here is about walking to his place of work where he was to raise up Lazarus. Raising the dead being part of his work while on earth was being threatened by plots by the priests to arrest him once he comes close to Jerusalem, yet Bethany the town of Lazarus was close to Jerusalem. Significant to see here is Jesus' concept of diligence.

• The presence of extra light in you must be a motivation to work more. A believer has extra hours of light so to say than an unsaved, which gives you more room to be productive. When being a Christian becomes a hindrance to diligence and productivity, the light within has gone dim.
.

• No threat should be strong enough to shut you in away from diligence.

> The lazy person claims, "There's a lion out there! If I go outside, I might be killed". Proverbs 22:13. (NLT).

The lion of the discouraging fellow worker or boss, tax collector, bad government and as many as you can think of must not take the virtue of diligence from you. Anything worth doing at all is truly worth doing well is applicable here.

CHAPTER 14

THE VALUE OF PATIENCE

Patience is the second occupier of the element of time that lies between seed and harvest.

> Therefore, be patient, brethren, until the coming of the Lord. See how the farmer waits for the precious fruit of the earth, waiting patiently for it until it receives the early and latter rain. James 5:7

Patience entails being persistent and being consistent in what you are doing till you see the desired result. 'Get rich quick' is no good enterprise. Many people have been conned of their hard earned money because someone promised them a short cut that can bypass the unavoidable route of patience in enterprise building. Every 'get rich quick scheme' being advertised on earth are scam, with no exemption, to make money for the scammers only. Think about it, if someone knows what you can do to make quick money, he or she would rather do it by him or herself.

- Patience will help you build your enterprise character.
- Patience will help you prove the system.
- Patience helps you to expand the dream within as growth itself needs time.
- Patience allows the unavoidable forces of nature to have their ways and take effect.
- Patience helps you to fine tune and evolve your skill.
- Patience helps you avoid many fatalities on the enterprise highway.

Most health and safety policies of this world are anchored on the premise of someone not being too much in a hurry to overlook potential danger. It is the same way it goes for enterprise development; it is safe to be patient.

CHAPTER 15

THE VALUE OF CONTINUOUS SEEDING

Noah did not plant and reap once and for all, he only 'began' to be a farmer in *Genesis 9:20*. His success as a farmer is anchored on his continuous farming. Continuous farming in this case is in continuous making provision for seed. Serious farmers chose the best of their produce and reserve such as seed. Continuous seeding is the guarantee for enlargement of ventures or a great future.

Major organisations across the world spend a lot of money on two areas that guarantee ever improving performance for them in the market.

• **_Products Development and Improvement:_** Huge amount of money goes into researches on products and service delivery by major market players. This huge money might look like waste to a non-discrete investor but for those who understand the concept of ever evolving elasticity of human needs, such is money well spent. Whenever you see an organisation that transcends generations and are still relevant, you have seen a sowing organisation. They spent time, money and energy to evolve their products in goods and services. They spend time energy and money to break new grounds in product and services delivery.

• **_Personnel Development and Improvement:_** Because we live in a human world, the humans behind the goods, services or skills is so important to enterprise development. Having the right products in goods or services is not enough; having the right skills for delivery is not enough either. Being and having the right person doing the delivery is what brings out the value.

Whereas products development deals with _'thing'_ such as goods, services and skills development to meet the market needs, personnel development and improvement deals with the _'person'_ who is delivering the goods, services or skills. The former deals with the capacity development in enterprise charisma, while the latter deals with the development of the enterprise character. Improving your person ultimately improves your market value. *Whether as an employee, a partner or an employer, the lee way of getting away with poor personality at work is very narrow.* Poor personality will always tell on and stand in the way of your enterprise development. Whether you will learn character by training for performance or develop it as a habit to keep, you will still need it either way.

Continuous seeding is what makes a farmer, not just a once in a while or once and for all seeding. How long it took Noah's farm to become big enough to build a winery alongside it we don't know, but we know that he began to be a farmer and he continued being one till his vine was big enough to build a winery. The value in seeding is that you don't consume all of your profits. Set a substantial part aside and plough it back in for continuous growth and investment. Give priority to products and services developments and improvement researches. Give more priority to personnel, personality and personal evolvement both in skill and organisational character. Make it an enterprise value and ideal to be respected by all that would be part of it and the future shall be guaranteed.

Some Salient Points to Consider:

- Value stands out your enterprise in volatile enterprise market of life.
- As long as the earth remains the cycle of seeding, time of diligence and then harvest remain.
- Every valuable enterprise character is built in patience.
- Human development is as important and even more than products and skill development.

CHAPTER 16

WISDOM OF STAYING IN THE PLACE OF INSPIRATION

Why wisdom? Because it takes wisdom of a kind to have resounding success against all odds. How did we know that Noah had wisdom? We do because Noah had resounding success and his account of success was found in God's wisdom book. His name was also included in God's hall of fame of those who did well in their generations.

On a deeper consideration:

> Through skillful and godly Wisdom is a house
> (a life, a home, a family) built, and by understanding
> it is established [on a sound and good foundation], and by

knowledge shall its chambers [of every area] be filled with all precious and pleasant riches. Proverbs 24:3-4. (AMP).

Skillful and godly wisdom is required in successful building of any enterprise, whether public or private. A First Class certificate from the best university in the world without skillful and godly wisdom will only result in an empty life of servitude and frustration. Wisdom is a major leverage for success; Noah had it and came up with good success. There are three simple streams of wisdom Noah saw which you too can see and leverage upon.

The Place of Inspiration

When Noah came out of the ark, the first thing he did was that he built an altar as a token of his link with higher wisdom, even the wisdom of God. It was at this altar of sacrifice that Noah picked his business inspiration from the heart of God. He needed a profound answer to the nagging question of how else seeds can be preserved and spread abroad in a controlled manner outside leaving them to birds and nature for proliferation by chance. And then suddenly, Noah heard God saying something along the lines of seeds becoming fruits by deliberate subjecting them to the process of time. The issue here is that God was not saying so audibly. God was saying it in His own heart and Noah picked it. Inspiration along the right path comes automatically, if by any chance you have access to the mind of God.

> Then Noah built an altar to the LORD, and took of every clean animal and of every clean bird, and offered burnt offerings on the altar. And the LORD smelled a soothing aroma. Then the LORD said in His heart, "I will never again curse the ground for man's sake, although the imagination of man's heart is evil from his youth; nor will I again destroy every living thing as I have done. While the earth remains, seedtime and harvest, cold and heat, winter and summer, and day and night shall not cease. Genesis 8:20-22.

As well abused as this passage of the Bible might have been, it is the open door of ideas into Noah's farming enterprise. Truly Noah gave God some sacrifice here, but what Noah got in return was massive farming idea. He didn't get a passage to quote in order to force money out of people's pockets; he got what he himself must put into practice in order to enrich himself and the earth. He learnt the practice of practical and deliberate sowing of seeds for anticipated harvest.

Noah was inspired to put effort up as seed wherever he intends to reap harvest in return. Noah would probably have been thinking of what next to do after coming out of the ark, but he decided to do the altar business first. Then suddenly as God spoke to Himself at the altar, Noah picked it as divine signal. God didn't ask Noah to be a farmer directly but Noah picked it by inspiration. What of if Noah did not build an altar. God would not have smelled a sweet savour and probably wouldn't have said what he said in His own heart for Noah's sake.

Noah also learnt from the heart of God that wickedness and evil tendencies will continue on the earth here for as long as the earth is being inhabited by man. But more importantly did he learn that the wickedness is not a valid excuse for not doing well in your own personal enterprise. It is never going to be a perfect and evil-free world, but you don't really need one as such to prosper. Many of us have not venture into productive living we dream of in our heart simply because of the evil that others do. That is a wrong inspiration, as God himself said that in spite of the evil, productivity will continue as long as the law of input and output of seeds and fruits respectively in their various forms is observed.

The evil of men will not stop the law of productivity, just as it will not stop the law of time and season. This is the reason why we have many non-churched, non-believing or even morally unsound people who are doing greatly well in their enterprises on the earth. They know that in spite of their imperfections, if they can put up a good effort as seed, the law of harvest says with time they will reap harvest in that same path. Noah was righteous but he knew that the seed of righteousness will not grow until it goes under the ground and become fruits of grapes. From what was said in God's heart above, seed can be the following and even many more, depending of what fruit you desire:

- *Seed of efforts in hard work for fruit of success.*
- *Material seeds towards God's cause and work on the earth for the fruit blessing from heaven.*
- *Material seed of benevolence towards the needy for fruit of help in your own time of need.*
- *Idea seed towards fruit of productivity.*
- *Seed of goodwill in kindness for fruit of same in return.*
- *Seed of physical and mental service unto God's kingdom for fruits of crowns and rewards in their various forms.*
- *Seed of service unto other humanity's causes for fruit of relevance and attending happiness.*
- *Time seed in getting all of the above done and time fruit in enjoying the rewards they bring.*

Noah picked up the first and the last ones; he sowed the

seed of effort and hard work in planting grapes, and he gave it time and had a good harvest of vine for wine.

Your wisdom is to stay in the place of inspiration, which is where you will have access to the winning wisdom of God for your triumph in the market place of life. Your place of inspiration ranges from the direct house and presence of God to other places, associations and scenes you hardly pay attention to. The truth is that God wants to inspire his own with wisdoms, and he will use all available opportunities in life to inspire you. He will use places, persons or things:

(I)   *Personal communion with God* is your first place of inspiration. The altar of God must be built and always on fire in the recess of your spirit and mind. There will God inspire you and generate ideas and godly wisdom for you within to go about the business of life.

(ii)   *The house of God* which is literally the Church is your next major place of inspiration. God speaks in seasons and times and the Church is his headquarters of operation on earth. He therefore announces the seasons and times to His own as they come to his presence as a congregation.

(iii) *Wise company* you spend time with can and should

be a place of inspiration for you. When you spend time in wise company, you get inspired, challenged and pushed from inside with extra energy and ideas to pursue productivity. Any company that pushes you the other way round is wrong company.

(iv) *Trainings, seminars, conferences* and other productivity enhancing gatherings as such can also serve as your place of inspiration. You will get challenged, hear of new trends and idea and learn better ways of going about your enterprise pursuit. Mere seeing and hearing from those who are doing well in their own pursuits should spur you into productive pursuits too. They are necessarily not and must not be mistaken or substituted for church gathering by a believer. They are what they are and must be seen and benefited from as such.

(v) *Scenes and places* can inspire you. These can be scenes and places of interest that gives you the good feeling to think well along certain paths of productivity. They also can be bad scenes and places of challenges that inspire you into adamant desire for solutions from the inside.

(vi) *Events and experiences* in your past could be your place of inspiration. Introspection and retrospection can just inspire you into the wisdom for the next level and phase of your productive life.

All of the above can be your inspiration salvo of winning wisdom. You will just know what to do and how to do it and you will do it. As you do it, you will just prosper. The wisdom behind the wisdom of inspiration is for you to expose yourself to what can and will inspire you. Inspiration is what keeps pushing forward your expiration date. You cannot expire as long as you stay inspired. As long as you stay inspired, you will not be blunt or lag behind but stay sharp, relevant and up to date in the cutting edge of productive living.

"Inspiration is what keeps pushing forward your expiration date."

CHAPTER 17

TAKE YOUR CHANCE IN THE SCHEME

Life in itself is like a big amorphous scheme of times, seasons and events woven together which eventually make sense at the end. Many chances for you to play your part in the scheme will come up as what we call *'opportunities'*. Taking your own chance in the scheme is what we refer to as making most of your opportunity, and this is wisdom.

Different phases in the bigger scheme of things in human endeavour as have been already programmed by the higher power will present you with various opportunities to be part of the happenings. When you locate and occupy your own space in the happening, you get rewarded. Noah keyed into the agenda of heaven for the earth to be re-populated. Even before the then world and the inhabitants in animals, plants and humans were wiped off with flood, he heard God saying that the bigger scheme was not the destruction. He saw that the eventual agenda was to preserve species or seeds afterwards.

'Now that the flood was over, let the re-populating of everything begin', Noah would have said. He also heard God blessing him and his family and had a hint that

And the LORD said unto Noah, come thou and your entire house into the ark; for thee have I seen righteous before me in this generation...to keep seed alive upon the face of all the earth.
Genesis 7:1-3 (Abridged)

mankind had just been empowered by blessing to repopulate species on the earth, both of animals and plants, and Noah was not ready to miss the chance by not playing his own part.

When you refuse to be a mere spectator, complaining and commenting on how things are schemed so imperfectly without obvious lines of demarcations; when you are ready to just take your own chance and play your own part: you will succeed. Most people who suffer from and complain most about governing do not participate. Those who step out of constant complaining and participate reap the benefits of playing their parts. Same goes for every other enterprise. Play your part and get rewarded.

> I returned and saw under the sun that the race is not to the swift, nor the battle to the strong, nor bread to the wise, nor riches to men of understanding, nor favour to men of skill; but time and chance happen to them all.
> Ecclesiastes 9:11.

Your First Class degree in a field will not guarantee your share of the market in that field beyond the chance you see and take therein.

It is the Church's Time

This brings us to a very important issue with believers who are interested in building successful enterprises. I have very good news for you; your chance is here. By the scheme of things, this is Church age! It is the end time and the end time is the Church's time to dominate everywhere. It is Zion's prosperity season. The gospel of the kingdom must be preached in every nation now before the master comes, according to Jesus. *Matthew*

24:14. The kingdom of God will only be spread abroad though the prosperity of the kingdom itself; *Zechariah 1:17.* The end time Church is billed for success; literal success that will place her in the topmost top and you are part of it; *Isaiah 2:1-6.* Instead of fighting prosperity because many are abusing the concept, take your own chance in the scheme and use it rightly.

It is time for Church people to stand out and build mega corporations and also occupy prominent places of influence in already established ones. Your chance to build successful entrepreneurial enterprise has come, take it. All believers will not and are not supposed to be entrepreneurs but all are empowered to be successful in their fields of endeavour. The slogan of "I only like working for myself" could be an invitation to live and build mediocre corner shop enterprise whereas you were scheduled to head existing mega organisations. There is nothing wrong in working for others as long as you maximize your capacity. Joseph was working for the Egyptian government, but he was a mega success. Daniel worked for foreign kings in a strange land but he was a mega success. They all saw their chances in the bigger scheme that had already being prepared for a time as such and took it with both hands.

CHAPTER 18

TAKE YOUR TIME IN THE TIMING

We cannot talk of opportunities or chances and leave timing and time out of the equation of wisdom. Timing announces the season the scheme has been programmed for in life's agenda. Getting the timing right is not as difficult as getting your own time right. Within the timing are times, which are specific answers to 'when' in the whole schedule. *Whereas timing may only answer the question of 'what', time will answer of 'when'.*

I want to err on the side of caution now because the danger of jumping the gun simply because you know that the season or timing has come is high and risky. It was the season or timing of deliverance for Israel the moment Moses was born and Moses knew it. But Moses missed the time by ten years and put himself at serious risk of dying unsung at the backside of nowhere whereas he was meant for the forefront of everywhere. Moses' wrong timing added an extra thirty years of undoing the damage to the years of Israel in the house of bondage.

Wrong time in your timing of enterprise pursuit may lead to unemployment, indebtedness and many other attending bondage extensions. Taking Noah as our subject again. They just had a season of destruction which lasted for forty days and then came the timing of recovery. Once the rain stopped dropping on Noah's ark, he started planning the disembarking date, because the timing has come. This did not happen overnight, he waited for the right time in the timing. Noah didn't just open the door of his ark even when the flood had receded lest he got swept by residual flash. He had a very meticulous disembarking time table which I will like you to see in a simple but wise way from *Genesis 8:1-16;*

• The Rains from beneath and above stopped after 40 days
• The flood receded after 150 days which coincided with July 7th and the ark stopped moving – but Noah didn't

come out
- Water receded for another 3 months which coincided with October 1st – Noah only opened window to observe and saw the top of mountains.
- Noah waited for another 40 days and then sent out a raven – Noah didn't come out.
- Noah waited for another 7 days and sent a dove which came back with a twig – Noah didn't come out.
- Noah waited another 7 days which coincided with January 1st and sent another dove which found resting place for her feet and didn't come back into the ark – Noah removed the covering of the ark but remained in the ark.
- Noah waited for another 50 days which coincided with February 20th. – Noah came out.

Bearing any error margin of dating; Noah waited till the 340th day after the active flood has stopped for his time of coming out to happen, even though the timing of receding and recovery had come from day one after the end of the forty days of active flooding.

The wisdom is to always err on the side of caution when it comes to walking into your time within the timing. Many have gained pre-mature independence only to remain in bondage for the rest of their lives. Noah got his time right and God confirmed it by telling him to come out when he was ready to.

The issue with inspiration is that inspiration is pushy; you just want to go out there and get it done with. You just want to go out there and manifest your chance within the scheme. Time and chance has to be balanced with the wisdom of caution. It is very likely that one cannot be too cautious.

Lastly on the issue of time and timing, did you see it that Noah only 'began' to be a farmer in *Genesis 9:20*. How long it took him to get to the place of building his wine factory we were not told. The wisdom is that, whereas you can give yourself a dateline of when you want to start the enterprise adventure, do not put yourself under the pressure of dateline of anticipated landmarks in achievement. You may have seen those who did and it worked; it is not safe. The danger of discouragement and giving up is high when you set your timeline of anticipated achievement in matters that are not entirely within your control.

Noah's winning wisdom worked and the results justified it. You need wisdom for enterprise building justifiable by resounding success.

Watch the Harmony

There is a great deal to learn from an orchestra band when it comes to timing. The pleasantness of the piece being played is not just a function of the individual skills or even the togetherness in playing. It is rather the harmonization in what is being played. The timing of play is signified when the conductor standing in front of the players indicates so with his hand or baton. At this point everybody knows that it is time to play and is ready to play.

Nevertheless, individual players will still hold on and play nothing until it is time for such to bring in his or her own piece of sound into the music. While it is possible that the other players beside you have been playing their own notes and enjoying doing so for a while, the rule is that you will still wait till the music gets to where it needs your note and the conductor indicates so. Failure to observe this simple rule of waiting for your turn will disorganise the harmony no matter how skillfully you are playing.

The reality of orchestra is that you are not considered skillful by only knowing how to bring in your note but by knowing when to bring it in.

Many enterprise pursuits suffer from disorganised harmony simply because the person bearing the skill is not skillful enough to know the specific time to play his note within the general playing time. It is not about starting early or late, either can be wrong. It is about getting the balance in your time and timing. You cannot afford to jump ahead; neither should you lag behind. Personal application into knowing the right time is a vital practice that nobody else can do for you. There are conductor batons in life serving as pointers of when to start your note, change your tune or end the play. Others may still be playing even when you have been asked to stop playing; it is all about harmony of life.

Getting your time and timing right helps keep your enterprise life flow in a harmonious way. When harmony is lacking, one of the areas to check is not just what you are doing and how you are doing it. You may need to check when you are doing it as well.

Some Salient Points to Consider:

- Fruitful ideas have a habit of hanging around people and places of inspiration.
- The whole universe is like a lucrative sport but only players get paid. Play your little part well in the big scheme.
- Time is the specific target in the massive field of timing, don't miss the spot.

CHAPTER 19

STARTup &GROWup

If there is any enterprise value that needs to be reinstated to this generation ever than before, it is the value of not just talking but doing. It is the value of not just thinking about it but the value of conceptualising it and then starting it. Many have wanted to build a career in a field for almost a decade now and have done nothing along the path of making it a reality. Many have wanted to change their career or earning channels for almost a decade but have done nothing to realise the dream. They only talk of plan to seek another path whenever they come across some challenges on whatever path they are currently walking on. Once the heat subsides and the challenge recedes, they continue along that same line of comfort zone till dream dies and the vision is obliterated.

Start Somewhere

One sin you must not be guilty of when you leave this world of enterprise is that *'you never started'*. Be accused by life of many things but do not be accused of not starting at all.

Many of us always come up with the frustration-laden question of *'where do I start?'* In other words, *'I don't know where to start'*. I have good news and a simple answer for you. Life will never leave you without a starting point, except you fail or refuse to acknowledge it. The first and simple place for everyone in successful enterprise pursuit is the place of *'your immediate need'*. As simple as this piece sounds, it is the easiest way not to miss out on starting.

Therefore, to answer your question of where to start, I need to ask you the simple question: what is your immediate need? The answer to this question is the answer you have being seeking all these while. *Start from the place of your immediate need*. Our needs are always many and could be vague, but our immediate need(s) are always the pointer to where to start. You may want to build a very lofty enterprise in legal business, the first question is to appraise your present position and see your immediate need. In this case, it may be to acquire legal education and so schooling is the immediate need. If you are already studying something else, changing to legal studies is the immediate need. Your millennial journey into your desired world of enterprise starts with the steps you take towards meeting the immediate need along that path.

Your immediate need may be to be able to pay your basic bills which include feeding, clothing and shelter. Whatever legitimate engagement you throw yourself into to meet those first is your starting point. Your immediate need may be further education, professional training, job applications, apprenticeship, or debt settlement and so on. The reason to start there is because until you take the immediate step, what lies ahead to be done will remain a mystery that will never unravel. In certain instances, your immediate need might simply be the desire to find expression for what lies in your inside.

Noah started with his immediate need for fruits and then planted to get grape fruits. Even though he became so successful such that he started a winery, it all started with that simple immediate need for fresh fruits. You may need to first seek the 'just enough' phase of life even though you are planning for a conglomerate.

No Big Bang

One of the easy traps young people fall into when it comes into building a successful career or enterprise is the crave and desire to start with a 'big bang'. Except you are God, you may not have to start with a big bang. Not starting with a big bang nevertheless does not mean you cannot finish with a flourish. Being a young man, I always wanted to start big too; I always want all things to be in place while I start. Over time, I have realised that those who flourish and remain in the game are necessarily not those who started with a big bang. Noah started by beginning to be a farmer, not even as an entrepreneur. Simply a farmer, period.

The material capital for a big bang in starting may elude you forever, start with a small pinch. You may not be given a big bang of chance or big platform of expression to start with; start anyway and anyhow. It takes mental laziness and lack of wisdom of some sort to always want to start big. Your colleague may have it bigger than you at the start, but we will not all have the same size of privilege to start with. This is the true reality of life. Instead of bemoaning and comparing, you had better start somewhere now.

> Though your beginning
> was small, yet your
> latter end would increase
> abundantly.
> Job 8:7

Rather Start and Fail

I know failure is not desirable and failing is not a virtue, but I will rather you start and fail than wishing and hoping without starting for ever. Failing itself is the ultimate lasting cure for failure. Most people and organisations that succeed exceedingly in their pursuits are individuals and organisations that had to deal with the pain of failure at one point or the other. Failure helps you hone in your skills and makes you see the pain and price of failing. These last two may be the only motivations you need to do everything it takes to do it right and succeed.

Failing, like a pathogen, itself is not the medicine but the immunity to failure you develop as wisdom while failing is of great benefit. At times you do not fail because you did not do enough, but you did because of external factors you have not mastered. Microsoft Windows are so successful in the computer world today that hardly is there any user of computers who have not used one version or the other before. Coupled with years of delay in schedule of release and failure to dominate the market as expected, the release of the early version of Windows could not be called a success. *Failure on the known path in a career might be all you need to find and pioneer the unknown path.*

Grow Up

Starting up against all odds is a good virtue, but growing up till you get to the very top is a better one.

And Noah began to be a farmer. Genesis 9:20a.

The open end description with which Noah's enterprise pursuit was captured here is informative. The next verse of the same scripture showed a man that grew successful almost to the point of being drunk in his success. Because Noah's being drunk is not the focus here, we need to lay emphasis on the progress and growth his farming enterprise would have encountered to get to that point. Life's chance and opportunities can be so far and in between that whenever you are given yours, you need to maximize it. There is no more exploitation you can do with any chance given to you than how much you grow therein.

Growth is not an all-pleasant experience for even our physical body. Growth is what brings and results in the dreadful phenomenon we call ageing. Growth will stretch you beyond your imagination. Growth may involve several evolvements with their accompanying misunderstandings by those not experiencing same kind of growth. Growth may involve adding to your pace, thereby being separated from the familiar company. Growth must be craved and pursued with all tenacities and ferocities by those who don't want to settle for average.

> "Growth is what brings and results in the dreadful phenomenon we call ageing."

Where is Our Noah?

Every generation needs a Noah in one field and the other. Men and women who will evolve ideas to meet the current and evolving needs of mankind. We need men and women who will not just begin to be something but those who will grow up therein as well. We also need men and women of unlimited possibilities. We need men and women who will not just find and celebrate grace; we need those who will do something tangible with it. We need men and women who will build arks ahead of and in times of flood and plant vineyards ahead of and in time of harvest. We need multi-faceted and multi-talented men and women like Noah in our days too. We need those who will not just pray but who will do something after praying.

We need believers who will succeed and last in success so much that their legacies will have to be traced with carbon dating long after they have gone, if the Lord Jesus tarries.

The big question is: *'are you such a man as Noah?'*

Some salient points to note:
- You have not given yourself a chance of achieving until you start.
- Start big may never happen, but grow big is always available.
- Better to start and fail than failing to start.
- Don't just escape the flood, make the dry ground produce for you.

www.ingramcontent.com/pod-product-compliance
Lightning Source LLC
Chambersburg PA
CBHW060208070426
42447CB00035B/2855